Principles of
Biblical Interpretation

(SACRED HERMENEUTICS)

by

L. BERKHOF, B. D.

President Emeritus of Calvin Seminary
Grand Rapids, Michigan

BAKER BOOK HOUSE

GRAND RAPIDS   MICHIGAN

PHOTOLITHOPRINTED BY CUSHING - MALLOY, INC.
ANN ARBOR, MICHIGAN, UNITED STATES OF AMERICA
1973

PREFACE

Much of the present day confusion in the realm of religion, and in the application of Biblical principles, stems from distorted interpretation and misinterpretation of God's Word. That is true even in those circles which adhere unwaveringly to the infallibility of Holy Scriptures.

We are convinced that the adoption and use of sound principles of interpretation in the study of the Bible will prove surprisingly fruitful. We believe that this is one means which "the Spirit of truth" is pleased to use in leading His people "into all truth." It is with this in mind that we offer this book for individual guidance in the study of Scriptures, and particularly for use in seminaries and Bible schools. The early adoption of valid procedure in Biblical interpretation will lead the devoted kingdom worker to a life of useful service for the advancement of God's kingdom.

THE PUBLISHERS

Contents

Principles of
Biblical Interpretation

I. Introduction

The word *Hermeneutics* is derived from the Greek word HERMENEUTIKE which, in turn, is derived from the verb HERMENEUO. Plato was the first to employ HE HERMENEUTIKE (sc. TECHNE) as a technical term. Hermeneutics is, properly, the art of TO HERMENEUEIN, but now designates the theory of that art. We may define as follows: *Hermeneutics is the science that teaches us the principles, laws, and methods of interpretation.*

We must distinguish between *general* and *special* Hermeneutics. The former applies to the interpretation of all kinds of writings; the latter to that of certain definite kinds of literary productions, such as laws, history, prophecy, poetry. *Hermeneutica Sacra* has a very special character, because it *deals with* a book that is unique in the realm of literature, viz., with *the Bible as the inspired Word of God.* It is only when we recognize the principle of the divine inspiration of the Bible that we can maintain the theological character of Hermeneutica Sacra.

Hermeneutics is usually studied with a view to the interpretation of the literary productions of the past. Its special task is to point out the way in which the differences or the distance between an author and his readers may be removed. It teaches us that this is properly accomplished only by the readers' transposing themselves into the time and spirit of the author. In the study of the Bible, it is not sufficient that we understand the meaning of the secondary authors (Moses,

11

Isaiah, Paul, John, etc.) ; we must learn to know the mind of the Spirit.

The *necessity* of the study of hermeneutics follows from several considerations:

(1) *Sin darkened the understanding of man, and still exercises a pernicious influence on his conscious mental life.* Therefore, special efforts must be made to guard against error.

(2) *Men differ from one another in many ways that naturally cause them to drift apart mentally.* They differ, for instance,

(a) in intellectual capacity, aesthetic taste, and moral quality resulting in a lack of spiritual affinity:

(b) in intellectual attainment, some being educated, and others uneducated; and

(c) in nationality, with a corresponding difference in language, forms of thought, customs, and morals.

The study of Hermeneutics is *very important* for future ministers of the Gospel, because:

(1) The intelligent study of the Bible only will furnish them with the material which they need for the construction of their theology.

(2) Every sermon they preach ought to rest on a solid exegetical foundation. This is one of the greatest desiderata of the present day.

(3) In instructing the young people of the Church, and in family visitation, they are often called upon unexpectedly to interpret passages of Scripture. On such occasions, a fair understanding of the laws of interpretation will aid them materially.

(4) It will be a part of their duty to defend the truth over against the assaults of higher criticism. But in order to do this effectively, they must know how to handle it.

In the Encyclopaedia of Theology, Hermeneutics belongs to the Bibliological group of studies, that is, to those studies that center about the Bible. It naturally follows the *Philologia Sacra,* and immediately precedes *Exegesis.* Hermeneutics and Exegesis are related to each other as theory and practice. The one is a science, the other an art.

In this study on Hermeneutics, we deem it necessary to include the following in the order here given:

(1) A brief outline of the history of Hermeneutical principles. The past may teach us many things both negatively and positively.

(2) A description of those characteristics of the Bible that determine, in measure, the principles that are to be applied in its interpretation.

(3) An indication of the qualities that should characterize, and of the requirements that are essential in an interpreter of the Bible.

(4) A discussion of the threefold interpretation of the Bible, namely,

(a) *the Grammatical,* including the logical interpretation;

(b) *the Historical,* including also the psychological interpretation; and

(c) *the Theological* interpretation.

QUESTIONS: What is the difference between Hermeneutics and Exegetics? Are general and special Hermeneutics mutually exclusive or does the one in some sense include the other? In what respect did sin disturb the mental life of man? Why should we apply a threefold interpretation to the Bible?

LITERATURE: Immer. *Hermeneutics,* pp. 1-14; Elliott, *Biblical Hermeneutics,* pp. 1-7; Terry, *Biblical Hermeneutics,* pp. 17-22; Lutz, *Biblische Hermeneutik,* pp. 1-14.

II. History of Hermeneutical Principles
Among the Jews

A. Definition of History of Hermeneutics

We must distinguish between the history of Hermeneutics as a science and the history of Hermeneutical principles. The former would have to begin with the year 1567 A.D., when Flacius Illyricus made the first attempt at a scientific treatment of Hermeneutics; while the latter takes its start at the very beginning of the Christian era.

A history of Hermeneutical principles seeks to answer three questions;

(1) *What was the prevailing view respecting the Scriptures?*

(2) *What was the prevalent conception of the method of interpretation?*

(3) *What qualifications were regarded as essential in an interpreter of the Bible?*

The first two questions are of a more perennial character than the last one, and naturally require a greater amount of attention.

B. Principles of Interpretation among the Jews

For the sake of completeness, a brief statement is given of the principles which the Jews applied in the interpretation of the Bible. The following classes of Jews must be distinguished.

1. THE PALESTINIAN JEWS. These had a profound respect for the Bible as the infallible Word of God. They regarded even the letters as holy, and their copyists were in the

habit of counting them, lest any of them should be lost in transcription. At the same time, they held the Law in far greater esteem than the *Prophets* and the *Holy Writings*. Hence the interpretation of the Law was their great objective. They carefully distinguished between the mere literal sense of the Bible (technically called *peshat*) and its exposition of exegesis (*midrash*). "One controlling motive and feature of midrash was to investigate and elucidate, by all exegetical means at command, all possible hidden meanings and applications of Scripture" (Oesterley and Box, *The Religion and worship of the Synagogue*, p. 75.f.). In a broad sense, the Midrashic literature may be divided into two classes:

(a) interpretations of a legal character, dealing with matters of binding law in a strict legalistic sense (*Halakhah*), and

(b) interpretations of a free and more edifying tendency, covering all the non-legal parts of Scripture (*Haggadah*). The latter were homiletical and illustrative rather than exegetical.

One of the great weaknesses of the interpretation of the Scribes is due to the fact that it exalted the *Oral Law*, which is, in the last analysis, identical with the inferences of the rabbis, as a necessary support of the *Written Law*, and finally used it as a means to set the Written Law aside. This gave rise to all manner of arbitrary interpretation. Notice the verdict of Christ in Mark 7:13.

Hillel was one of the greatest interpreters of the Jews. He left us seven rules of interpretation by which, at least in appearance, oral tradition could be deduced from the data of the Written Law. These rules, in their briefest form, are as follows: (a) *light and heavy* (that is, a *minore ad majus,* and vice versa); (b) *"equivalence"*; (c) *deduction from special to general;* (d) *an inference from several passages;* (e) *in-*

ferences from the general to the special; (f) *analogy from another passage; and* (g) *an inference from the context.*

2. THE ALEXANDRIAN JEWS. Their interpretation was determined more or less by the philosophy of Alexandria. *They adopted the fundamental principle of Plato that one should not believe anything that is unworthy of God.* And whenever they found things in the Old Testament that did not agree with their philosophy and that offended their sense of propriety, they resorted to allegorical interpretations. Philo was the great master of this method of interpretation among the Jews. He did not altogether reject the literal sense of Scripture, but regarded it as a concession to the weak. For him, it was merely a symbol of far deeper things. The hidden meaning of Scripture was the all-important one. He, too, left us some principles of interpretation. *"Negatively,* he says that the literal sense must be excluded when anything is stated that is unworthy of God;—when otherwise a contradiction would be involved;—and when Scripture itself allegorizes. *Positively,* the text is to be allegorized, when expressions are doubled; when superfluous words are used; when there is a repetition of facts already known; when an expression is varied; when synonyms are employed; when a play of words is possible in any of its varieties; when words admit of a slight alteration; when the expression is unusual; when there is anything abnormal in the number or tense" (Farrar, *History of Interpretation,* p. 22). These rules naturally opened the way for all kinds of misinterpretations. For examples, cf. Farrar, *History,* p. 139 ff.; Gilbert, *Interpretation of the Bible,* pp. 44-54.

3. THE KARAITES. This sect, designated by Farrar "the Protestants of Judaism," was founded by Anan ben David about 800 A.D. With a view to their fundamental characteristic, they may be regarded as the spiritual descendants of the

Sadducees. They represent a protest against Rabbinism that was partly influenced by Mohammedanism. The Hebrew form of the word "Karaites" is Beni Mikra—"Sons of reading." They were so called because *their fundamental principle was to regard Scripture as the sole authority in matters of faith.* This meant, on the one hand, a disregard of oral tradition and of rabbinical interpretation, and, on the other, a new and careful study of the text of Scripture. In order to refute them, the Rabbis undertook a similar study, and the outcome of this literary conflict was the Massoretic text. Their exegesis was, on the whole, far sounder than that of either the Palestinian or Alexandrian Jews.

4. THE CABBALISTS. The Cabbalist movement of the twelfth century was of a far different nature. It really represents the *reductio ad absurdum* of the method of interpretation employed by the Jews of Palestine, though it also employed the allegorical method of the Alexandrian Jews. They proceeded on the assumption that the whole Massorah, even down to the verses, words, letters, vowel-points and accents, was delivered to Moses on Mount Sinai; and that the "numbers of the letters, every single letter, the transposition, the substitution, had a special, even a supernatural power." In their attempt to unlock the divine mysteries, they resorted to the following methods:

(a) *Gematria,* according to which they could substitute for a given biblical word another that had the same numerical value;

(b) *Notarikon,* which consisted in forming words by the combination of initial and terminal letters, or by regarding each letter of a word as the initial letter of other words; and

(c) *Temoorah,* denoting a method of evolving new meanings by an interchange of letters. For examples, cf. Farrar, p. 98ff.;

Gilbert, p. 18ff.

5. THE SPANISH JEWS. From the twelfth to the fifteenth centuries, a more healthy method of interpretation developed among the Jews of Spain. When the exegesis of the Christian Church was at a low ebb, and the knowledge of Hebrew was almost lost, a few learned Jews on the Pyrenaean Peninsula restored the light to the candlestick. Some of their interpretations are quoted up to the present day. The principal exegete among them were Abr. Aben-Ezra, Sal. Izaak Jarchi, David Kimchi, Izaak Aberbanel, and Elias Levita. From these Jewish scholars, Nicolas de Lyra and Reuchlin received great aid.

QUESTIONS: How did Rabbinical Judaism conceive of the inspiration of the Bible? Why did the Jews ascribe unique significance to the Law? What did they teach about the origin of the Oral Law? How did it really originate, and of what did it consist? What is the Mishnah? the Gemara? the Talmud? How does the Jewish use of tradition compare with that of the Roman Catholics? What is the difference between an allegory and allegorical interpretation? What is the Massorah? How must we account for the Cabbalistic movement? Did the Jewish interpreters of the fifteenth century affect the Reformation in any way?

LITERATURE: Diestal, *Geschichte des Alten Testaments,* pp. 6-14, 197-208; Ladd, *The Doctrine of Sacred Scriptures,* p. 691 ff.; Farrar, *History of Interpretation,* pp. 17-158; Gilbert, *Interpretation of the Bible,* pp. 1-57; Terry, *Biblical Hermeneutics,* pp. 31-35.

III. History of Hermeneutical Principles in the Christian Church

A. The Patristic Period

In the patristic period the development of Hermeneutical principles is connected with three different centers of Church life.

1. THE SCHOOL OF ALEXANDRIA. At the beginning of the third century A.D., biblical interpretation was influenced especially by the catechetical school of Alexandria. This city was an important seat of learning, where Jewish religion and Greek philosophy met and influenced each other. The Platonic philosophy was still current there in the forms of Neo-Platonism and Gnosticism. And it is no wonder that the famous catechetical school of this city came under the spell of the popular philosophy and accommodated itself to it in its interpretation of the Bible. It found the natural method for harmonizing religion and philosophy at hand in the allegorical interpretation, for

(a) Pagan philosophers (Stoics) had already for a long time applied that method in the interpretation of Homer, and thereby pointed out the way; and

(b) Philo who was also an Alexandrian, lent to this method the weight of his authority, reduced it to a system, and applied it even to the simplest narratives.

The chief representatives of this school were Clement of Alexandria and his disciple, Origen. They both regarded the Bible as the inspired Word of God, in the strictest sense, and shared the opinion of the day that special rules had to be applied in the interpretation of divine communications. And while they recognized the literal sense of the Bible, they were of the opinion that only the allegorical interpretation contributed to real knowledge.

Clement of Alexandria was the first one to apply the allegorical method to the interpretation of the New Testament as well as to that of the Old. He *propounded the principle that all Scripture must be understood allegorically.* This was a step in advance of other Christian interpreters, and constitutes the chief characteristic of Clement's position. According to him, the literal sense could only furnish an elementary faith, while the allegorical sense led on to true knowledge.

His disciple, *Origen,* surpassed him in both learning and influence. He was, no doubt, the greatest theologian of his age. But his abiding merit lies in his work in textual criticism rather than in biblical interpretation. "As an interpreter, he illustrated the Alexandrian type of exegesis most systematically and extensively" (Gilbert). In one of his works, he furnished a detailed theory of interpretation. The *fundamental principle* of this work *is, that the meaning of the Holy Spirit is always simple and clear and worthy of God. All that seems dark and immoral and unbecoming in the Bible simply serves as an incentive to transcend or pass beyond the literal sense.* Origen regarded the Bible as a means for the salvation of man; and because, according to Plato, man consists of three parts—body, soul, and spirit—he accepted a threefold sense, namely *the literal, the moral,* and *the mystical or allegorical sense.* In his exegetical praxis, he rather disparaged the literal sense of Scripture, referred but seldom to the moral sense, and constantly employed allegory—since only it yielded true knowledge.

2. THE SCHOOL OF ANTIOCH. The school of Antioch was probably founded by Dorotheus and Lucius towards the end

of the third century, though Farrar regards Diodorus, first presbyter of Antioch, and after 378 A.D. bishop of Tarsus, as the real founder of the school. The latter wrote a treatise on principles of interpretation. But his greatest monument consisted of his two illustrious disciples, Theodore of Mopsuestia and John Chrysostom.

These two men differed greatly in every respect. Theodore held rather liberal views respecting the Bible, while John regarded it as being in every part the infallible Word of God. The exegesis of the former was intellectual and dogmatic; that of the latter, more spiritual and practical. The one was famous as a critic and interpreter; the other, though an exegete of no mean ability, eclipsed all his contemporaries as a pulpit orator. Hence, *Theodore* was styled *the exegete,* while *John* was called *Chrysostom* (the golden-mouthed) for the splendor of his eloquence. *They went far towards the development of true scientific exegesis, recognizing, as they did, the necessity of determining the original sense of the Bible,* in order to make a profitable use of it. Not only did they attach great value to the literal sense of the Bible, but they consciously rejected the allegorical method of interpretation.

In the work of exegesis, Theodore surpasses Chrysostom. He had an open eye for the human factor in the Bible, but, sorry to say, denied the divine inspiration of some of the Scriptural books. Instead of the allegorical, he defended the *grammatico-historical interpretation,* in which he was far in advance of his time. And though he recognized the typical element in the Bible, and found Messianic passages in some of the Psalms, he explained most of them *zeitgeschichtlich.* The three Cappadocians belonged to this school.

3. THE WESTERN TYPE OF EXEGESIS. A mediating type of exegesis made its appearance in the West. It harbored some elements of the allegorical school of Alexandria, but

also recognized some of the principles of the Syrian school. Its most characteristic feature, however, is found in the fact that *it advanced another element, which had not asserted itself up to that time, namely, the authority of tradition and of the Church in the interpretation of the Bible.* Normative value was ascribed to the teaching of the Church in the sphere of exegesis. This type of exegesis was represented by *Hilary* and *Ambrose;* but especially by *Jerome* and *Augustine.*

The fame of Jerome is based on his translation of the Vulgate, rather than on his interpretations of the Bible. He was familiar with both Hebrew and Greek, but his work in the exegetical field consists primarily of a large number of linguistic, historical, and archeological notes. Augustine differed from Jerome in that his knowledge of the original languages was very deficient. This is equivalent to saying that he was not primarily an exegete. He was great in systematizing the truths of the Bible, but not in the interpretation of Scripture. His Hermeneutical principles, which he worked out in his *De Doctrina Christiana,* were better than his exegesis. He demands that an interpreter shall be philologically, critically, and historically equipped for his task, and shall, above all, have love for his author. He stressed the necessity of having regard for the literal sense, and of basing the allegorical upon it; but, at the same time, he indulged rather freely in allegorical interpretation. Moreover, in cases where the sense of Scripture was doubtful, he gave a deciding voice to the *regula fidei* by which he meant a compendious statement of the faith of the Church. Sad to say, Augustine also adopted a fourfold sense of Scripture: *a historical, an aetiological, an analogical, and an allegorical* sense. And it was particularly in this respect that he influenced the interpretation of the Middle Ages.

QUESTIONS: What was the character of the early catechetical schools? What gave rise to the allegorical method of interpretation? How can you prove that the method is faulty? How did the Alexandrian school distinguish between *pistis and gnosis?* Did the Alexandrians recognize the human element in Scripture? What was the fundamental difference between the school of.Alexandria and that of Antioch? What was meant by the *regula fidei* in the early Church? Why is it a mistake to make the teaching of the Church the standard of exegesis?

LITERATURE: Diestel, *Geschichte des Alten Testaments*, pp. 16-148; Farrar, *History of Interpretation*, pp. 161-142; Gilbert, *Interpretation of the Bible*, pp. 108-145; Terry, *Biblical Hermeneutics*, pp. 35-44; Immer, *Hermeneutics*, pp. 31-36.

B. The Period of the Middle Ages

During the Middle Ages, many, even of the clergy, lived in profound ignorance of the Bible. And insofar as they knew it, it was only in the translation of the Vulgate, and through the writings of the Fathers. It was generally regarded as a book full of mysteries, which could be understood only in a mystical manner. *In this period,* the fourfold sense of Scripture (literal, tropological, allegorical, and analogical) was generally accepted, and it became an established principle that the *interpretation of the Bible had to adapt itself to tradition and to the doctrine of the Church.* It was considered to be the acme of wisdom to reproduce the teachings of the Fathers, and to find the teachings of the Church in the Bible. The rule of St. Benedict was wisely adopted in the monasteries, and decreed that the Scriptures should be read, and with them, as a final explanation, the exposition of the Fathers. Hugo of St. Victor even said: "Learn first what you should believe, and then go to the Bible to find it there." And in cases in which the interpretations of the Fathers differed, as they often did, the interpreter was in duty bound to choose, *quod ubique, quod semper, quod ab omnibus creditum est.* Not a single new Hermeneutical principle was developed at this time, and exegesis was bound hand and foot by traditional lore and by the authority of the Church.

This condition of things is clearly reflected in the works that were written during this period. The following are some of the most typical.

1. THE GLOSSA ORDINARIA *of Walafrid Strabo, and the* GLOSSA INTERLINEARIS *of Anselm of Laon. These were compilations of literal, moral, and mystical fragments, interspersed with grammatical remarks of a very elementary character.* The interpretations given are often of a contradictory nature, and therefore mutually exclusive; and in many cases it is left to the reader, with an *aliter,* or *potest etiam intelligi,* to choose between them. The Glosses of Walafrid Strabo were invested with high authority.

2. THE CATENAE, of which the most famous were those of *Procopius of Gaza in the East, and those of Thomas of Aquinas in the West.* In these we find *a collection of patristic interpretations strung together like a chain.* Their value naturally depended on the sources from which they were derived.

3. THE LIBER SENTENTIARUM *of Peter Lombard.* This work is mainly a *compilation of expositions, selected from the writings of Hilary, Ambrose, and Augustine.* But it differs from the works named above *in being more than a compilation.* While Peter the Lombard was careful not to transgress against the established authority on the side of independence, yet, within the prescribed limits, *he raised questions, made distinctions, and even added comments of his own.* In the immediately following centuries, his work was studied more diligently than the Bible itself.

While the fourfold sense of Scripture was generally accepted at this time (literal, tropological, allegorical, and anagogical), some at least began to see the incongruity of such a view. Even *Thomas Aquinas* seems to have felt it vaguely. It is true, he allegorizes constantly, but he also, *at least in theory, regarded the literal sense as the necessary foundation for all exposition of Scripture.* But it was especially *Nicolas of Lyra* that broke the fetters of his age. Ostensibly he did not abandon current opinion, even in its acceptance of a four-fold sense, but *in reality he admitted only two senses, the literal and the mystic, and even so founded the latter exclusively on the former.* He urged the necessity of referring to the original, complained about the mystic sense being "allowed to choke the literal," and demanded that the latter only should be used in proving doctrine. His work influenced Luther profoundly, and insofar also affected the Reformation.

Questions: What did the Church of the Middle Ages mean, when it spoke of tradition? What authority was ascribed to this tradition? What was the relation of Dogmatics to Exegesis in this period? What objections are there to this position? On what did the Church base its prerogative of determining the sense of Scripture? How did the theory of the fourfold sense originate?

Literature: Diestel, *Geschichte,* pp. 149-229; Farrar, *History,* pp. 245-303; Gilbert, *Interpretation,* pp. 146-180; Immer, *Hermeneutics,* pp. 36, 37; Davidson, *Sacred Hermeneutics,* pp. 155-192.

C. The Period of the Reformation

The Renaissance was of great importance for the development of sound Hermeneutical principles. In the fourteenth and fifteenth centuries, dense ignorance prevailed as to the contents of the Bible. There were doctors of divinity who had never read it through. And the only form in which the Bible was known at all was in the translation of Jerome. *The Renaissance called attention to the necessity of going back to the original.* Reuchlin and Erasmus—called the two eyes of Europe—came under its spell, and urged upon the interpreters of the Bible the duty of studying Scriptures in the languages in which they were written. Moreover, they greatly facilitated such study: the former by publishing a *Hebrew Grammar* and a *Hebrew Lexicon;* and the latter, by editing *the first critical edition of the New Testament in Greek.* The fourfold sense of Scripture was gradually abandoned, and the principle established that the Bible has but one sense.

The Reformers believed the Bible to be the inspired Word of God. But, however strict their conception of inspiration, they conceived of it as *organic* rather than *mechanical.* In certain particulars, they even revealed a remarkable freedom in handling Scriptures. At the same time, they regarded the Bible as the highest authority, and as the final court of appeal in all theological disputes. Over against the infallibility of the Church they placed the infallibility of the Word. Their position is perfectly evident from the statement *that the Church does not determine what the Scriptures teach, but the Scriptures determine what the Church ought to teach.* The essential character of their exegesis resulted from two fundamental principles: (1) *Scriptura Scripturae interpres,* that is, Scripture is the interpreter of Scripture; and (2) *omnis intellectus ac expositio Scripturae sit analogia fidei,* that is, let all understanding and exposition of Scripture be in conformity with the analogy of faith. And for them the *analogia fidei*=the *analogia Scripturae,* that is, the uniform teaching of Scripture.

1. LUTHER. He rendered the German nation a great service by translating the Bible into the German vernacular. He also engaged in the work of exposition, though only to a limited extent. His Hermeneutical rules were far better than his exegesis. Though he was not willing to recognize any but the literal sense, and scornfully spoke of the allegorical interpretation as *Affenspiel,* he did not entirely steer clear of the despised method. *He defended the right of private judgment; emphasized the necessity of taking the context and historical*

circumstances into account; demanded faith and spiritual insight in the interpreter; and desired to find Christ everywhere in Scripture.

2. MELANCHTHON. He was Luther's right hand and his superior in learning. His great talents and his extensive knowledge, also of Greek and Hebrew, were well adapted to make him an admirable interpreter. In his exegetical work, he proceeded on the sound principles that (a) *the Scriptures must be understood grammatically before they can be understood theologically; and* (b) *the Scriptures have but one certain and simple sense.*

3. CALVIN was, by common consent, the greatest exegete of the Reformation. His expositions cover nearly all the books of the Bible, and their value is still recognized. The fundamental principles of Luther and Melanchthon were also his, *and he surpassed them in making his practice square with his theory.* In the allegorical method he saw a contrivance of Satan to obscure the sense of Scripture. *He firmly believed in the typical significance of much that is found in the Old Testament,* but did not share the opinion of Luther that Christ should be found everywhere in Scripture. Moreover, *he reduced the number of Psalms that could be recognized as Messianic. He insisted on it that the prophets should be interpreted in the light of historical circumstances.* As he saw it, the chief excellency of an expositor consisted in *lucid brevity.* Moreover, *he regarded it as "the first business of an interpreter to let his author say what he does say, instead of attributing to him what we think he ought to say."*

4. THE ROMAN CATHOLICS. *These made no exegetical advance during the period of the Reformation.* They did not admit the right of private judgment, and defended, as over against the Protestants, the position that the Bible must be interpreted in harmony with tradition. The council of Trent

emphasized (a) *that the authority of ecclesiastical tradition must be maintained,* (b) *that the highest authority had to be ascribed to the Vulgate, and* (c) *that it is necessary to conform one's interpretation to the authority of the Church and to the unanimous consent of the Fathers.* Where these principles prevail, exegetical development has come to a dead stop.

QUESTIONS: What was the Renaissance? Was it a theistic or a humanistic movement? How did it influence the Reformation? What evidence have we that the Reformers had an organic conception of inspiration? How is it to be accounted for that at least the earlier Reformers did not altogether escape the danger of allegorizing? What is the "right of private judgment"? How did Melanchthon and Calvin propose to reach unanimity in the case of disputed interpretations? What is the only continuous and complete contribution of Luther to the exegesis of the New Testament? What is the character of Calvin's expositions? In what respects does his exegetical work mark an advance? Do Roman Catholic interpreters adhere strictly to the canons of Trent?

LITERATURE: Diestel, *Geschichte,* pp. 231-317; Farrar, *History,* pp. 307-354; Gilbert, *Interpretation,* pp. 181-223; Immer, *Hermeneutics,* pp. 37-42; Terry, *Biblical Hermeneutics,* pp. 46-50.

D. The Period of Confessionalism

During the period following the Reformation, it became evident that Protestants had not altogether purged out the old leaven. Theoretically, they retained the sound principle: *Scriptura Scripturae interpres.* But while they refused to subject their exegesis to the domination of tradition and of the doctrine of the Church as formulated by councils and popes, *they were in danger of leading it into bondage to the Confessional Standards of the Church.* It was preëminently the age of Confessions. "At one time almost every important city or principality had its own favorite creed" (Farrar). Moreover, it was a controversial period. Protestantism was woefully divided into several factions. The militant spirit of the age found expression in hundreds of polemical writings. Each one sought to defend his own opinion with an appeal to Scripture. *Exegesis became the handmaid of dogmatics, and degenerated into a mere search for proof-texts.* The Scriptures were studied in order to find there the truths that were embodied in the Confessions. This is particularly true of Lutheran, but in a measure also of Reformed theologians. It was during this period also that some inclined towards a mechanical conception of the inspiration of the Bible. Cf. the *Formula Consensus Helvetica.* The Buxtorfs held that even the vowels of the Hebrew texts were inspired.

The prevailing tendency of this period is not as significant for the history of Hermeneutical principles, as are some of the reactions against it. There are especially three that deserve mention.

1. THE SOCINIANS. They did not advance a single Hermeneutical principle, but in all their exposition proceeded on the assumption *that the Bible must be interpreted in a rational way, or—perhaps better—in harmony with reason.* As the Word of God it could not contain anything that was in contradistinction to reason, that is, according to them, *nothing that could not be rationally apprehended.* Thus the doctrines of the Trinity, of Providence, and of the two natures in Christ, went by the board. They constructed a theological system that consisted of a mixture of Rationalism and Supernaturalism. And while they gloried in their freedom from the Confessional yoke, their exegesis was, after all, dominated by their dogmatic system.

2. COCCEJUS. This Holland theologian was very much dissatisfied with the current method of interpretation. He felt that they who regarded the Bible as a collection of proof-texts, *failed to do justice to Scripture as an organism, of which the different parts were typically related to one another.* He demanded that the interpreter should study every passage in

the light of its context, of the prevailing thought, and of the purpose of the author.   His fundamental principle was *that the words of Scripture signify all that they can be made to signify in the entire discourse;* or, as he expresses it in one of his works: "the sense of the words in the Bible is so comprehensive that it contains more than one thought, yea, sometimes a multiplicity of thoughts, which an experienced interpreter of Scripture can deduce from it."   Thus, as Farrar says, "he introduced a false plurality of meanings, by a fatal confusion between the actual sense and all possible applications."   And this was aggravated by his *excessive typology, which induced him not only to seek Christ everywhere in the Bible, but also to find the vicissitudes of the New Testament Church, in the course of its history, typified in the Old Testament, and even in the words and deeds of Christ Himself.* But, however faulty his exegesis, he rendered good service by calling attention to the organic character of God's revelation.

J. A. Turretin opposed the arbitrary procedure of Coccejus and his followers.   Averse to the imaginary senses discovered by this school, he *insisted on it that the Bible should be interpreted without any dogmatic prepossessions, and with the aid of logic and analysis.*   He exercised a profound and beneficial influence.

3. THE PIETISTS.   Weary of the strife among Protestants, they were bent on promoting true piety of life.   On the whole, they represented a healthy reaction against the dogmatic interpretations of their day.   *They insisted on studying the Bible in the original languages, and under the enlightening influence of the Holy Spirit.* But the fact that, in their exposition, they aimed primarily at edification, gradually led to a contempt of science.   In their estimation, the *grammatical, historical, and analytical study of the Word of God merely fostered knowledge of the external husk of the divine thoughts, while the*

porismatic (drawing inferences for reproof, etc.) *and prac-tical* (praying and sighing) *study penetrated to the kernel of the truth.* Rambach and Francke were two of the most emi-nent representatives of this school. They were the first to urge the necessity of *psychological interpretation,* in the sense that the interpreter's feelings should be in harmony with those of the writer whom he wished to understand. The mystical tendencies of these interpreters led them to find special empha-ses where none existed. Bengel was the best interpreter which this school produced.

QUESTIONS: What important Confessions originated in this period? What vital objection is there to the domination of any Confession in the field of exegesis? What is the proper attitude of an inter-preter to the Confession of his Church? How is exegesis related to dogmatics? In what respects was Coccejus mistaken, and why? What is meant by psychological interpretation? Is piety necessary in an interpreter of the Bible?

LITERATURE: Diestel, *Geschichte,* pp. 317-554; Farrar, *History,* pp. 357-394; Gilbert, *Interpretation,* pp. 224-248; Reuss, *History of the New Testament,* pp. 572-586; Immer, *Hermeneutics,* pp. 42-54; Elliott, *Hermeneutics,* pp. 18-24.

E. The Historico-Critical Period

If the preceding period already witnessed some opposition to the dogmatical interpretation of the Bible, in the period now under consideration *the spirit of reaction gained the control-ling voice in the field of Hermeneutics and Exegesis.* It often found expression in very extreme positions, and then met with determined resistance. This period, too, was characterized by action and reaction. Widely divergent views were expressed respecting the inspiration of the Bible, but *they were all at one in the denial of verbal inspiration and of the infallibility of Scripture.* The human element in the Bible was stressed far more than ever before, and found general recognition; and they who also believed in the divine factor, reflected on the mutual relation of the human and the divine.

Attempts were now made to systematize the doctrine of inspiration. Some followed Le Clerk in *adhering to the theory of an inspiration varying in degrees in different parts of the Bible,* and in its lowest degrees admitting of errors and imperfections. Others accepted the theory of a *partial inspiration,* limiting it to those portions that pertain to faith and morals, and thus allowing for errors in historical and geographical matters. Schleiermacher and his followers *denied the supernatural character of inspiration,* and identified it with the spiritual illumination of Christians; while Wegscheider and Parker *reduced it to the power which all men possess simply in virtue of the light of nature.* In the present day, it is quite customary to speak of inspiration as *dynamic,* and to refer it to the authors rather than to their writings. According to Ladd, "it is to be conceived of as an incoming of supernatural and spiritual energy, which manifests itself in a heightened degree and new ordering of man's spiritual energy" (*The Doctrine of Sacred Scripture,* II, p. 471). The product of this is called "revelation."

It was represented as a *conditio sine qua non,* that the exegete should be *voraussetzungslos,* i.e., without prepossessions, and therefore entirely free from the domination of dogmatics and of the Confessional standards of the Church. Moreover, it became an established principle that *the Bible must be interpreted like every other book. The special divine element of the Bible was generally disparaged, and the interpreter usually limited himself to the discussion of historical and critical questions.* The abiding fruit of this period is the clear consciousness of the necessity of the *Grammatico-Historical* interpretation of the Bible. There are also evidences of a growing conviction that this twofold principle of interpretation must be supplemented by some other principle, in order that full justice may be done to the Bible as a divine revelation.

The beginning of this period was marked by the appearance of two opposite schools, the Grammatical and the Historical.

1. THE GRAMMATICAL SCHOOL. This school was founded by *Ernesti,* who wrote an important work on the interpretation of the New Testament, in which he *laid down four principles.* (a) *The manifold sense of Scripture must be rejected, and only the literal sense retained.* (b) *Allegorical and typological interpretations must be disapproved, except in cases where the author indicates that he meant to combine another sense with the literal.* (c) *Since the Bible has the grammatical sense in common with other books, this should be ascertained similarly in both cases.* (d) *The literal sense may not be determined by a supposed dogmatical sense.*

The Grammatical School was essentially supernaturalistic, binding itself to "the very words of the text as the legitimate source of authentic interpretation and of religious truth" (Elliott). But its method was one-sided in that it ministered only to a pure and simple interpretation of the text, which is not always sufficient in the interpretaton of the Bible.

2. THE HISTORICAL SCHOOL. The historical school originated with *Semler.* The son of pietistic parents, he became, more or less in spite of himself, the father of Rationalism. In his work on the Canon, he *directed attention to the neglected truth of the human historical origin and composition of the Bible.* And in a second work, on the interpretation of the New Testament, he laid down certain principles of interpretation. Semler stressed the fact that the various books of the Bible and the Canon as a whole originated in a historical way, *and were therefore historically conditioned.* From the fact that the separate books were written for different classes of

people, *he inferred that they contained much that was merely local and ephemeral, and that was not intended to have normative value for all men and at all times.* Moreover, *he saw in them an intermixture of error, since Jesus and the apostles accommodated themselves in some matters to the people whom they addressed.* Hence, he urged the necessity of bearing these things in mind in the interpretation of the New Testament. And in answer to the question as to just what is the element of binding truth in the Bible, he pointed to *"that which serves to perfect man's moral character,"* His teaching fostered the idea that the Scriptures are fallible human productions, and virtually made human reason the arbiter of faith. Semler did not originate these ideas, but simply made vocal the thoughts that were widely prevalent in his day.

3. RESULTANT TENDENCIES. While this period began with two opposite schools, it soon revealed *three distinct tendencies* in the field of Hermeneutics and Exegesis. A large number of interpreters developed the Rationalistic principles of Semler in a way that made him stand aghast. Others recoiled from the extreme positions of Rationalism, and either resorted to a mediating view, or reverted to the principles of the Reformation. Still others emphasized the fact that the Grammatico-Historical method of interpretation must be supplemented by some principle that would enable the expositor to penetrate into the spirit of Scripture.

a. *Rank Rationalism.* The seed sown by Semler was productive of rank Rationalism in the field of historical exposition. This may be seen from the following examples:

(1) *Paulus of Heidelberg assumed a purely naturalistic position.* He regarded "practical fidelity to reason" as the source of the Christian religion. Most notorious of all was his in-

terpretation of the miracles. He distinguished two questions, viz., (a) whether they occurred, and (b) how whatsoever occurred may have happened. And while he answered the former in the affirmative, he replied to the latter by discounting all the supernatural elements.

(2) The theory of Paulus was laughed to scorn by *Strauss,* who *proposed the mythical interpretation of the New Testament.* Under the influence of Hegel, he taught that the Messianic idea, with all its accretions of the miraculous, gradually developed in the history of humanity. In the time of Jesus, Messianic expectations were in the air. And his work and teaching left such a deep impression on his disciples, that, after his demise, they ascribed to him all the wonderful words and works, including the resurrection, that were expected of the Messiah.

(3) But this view, in turn, was ridiculed by *F. C. Baur,* the founder of Tuebingen school, who *taught that the New Testament originated according to the Hegelian principle of thesis, antithesis and synthesis.* He held that the hostility between the Petrine and Pauline parties led to the production of rival literature, and finally also to the composition of books that aimed at the reconciliation of the opposing parties. As a result, three tendencies are apparent in the New Testament literature. This theory has also had its day.

(4) At the present time, the Old Testament rather than the New Testament is the object of critical assaults. *The Graf-Kuenen-Wellhausen school aims at explaining the Old Testament in what is called "the objective historical" manner,* i.e., in harmony with an evolutionistic philosophy. Its work is characterized by a minuteness that excites admiration, and by great ingenuity; but there are even now signs that point to its passing character.

b. *Twofold reaction to Rationalism.*

Rationalism did not run its course without opposition. In course of time, a twofold reaction became apparent.

(1) *The Mediating School.* Though it can hardly be said that *Schleiermacher* founded this school, he was certainly its fountain-head. His posthumous work on Hermeneutics did not answer the general expectation. *He ignored the doctrine of inspiration, denied the permanent validity of the Old Testament, and treated the Bible like any other book.* Though he did not doubt the substantial genuineness of Scripture, he distinguished between *essentials* and *non-essentials,* and felt confident *that critical science was able to draw the line between the two.* With all his insistence on true piety of the heart, he followed, in his exegetical work, mainly the ways of Rationalism.

Some of his followers, such as De Wette, Bleek, Gesenius, and Ewald, *had decided leanings towards Rationalism.* But *others* were more evangelical, and followed a mediating course. Among these were Tholuck, Riehm, Weiss, Luecke, Neander, and others. They *rejected entirely the theory of a verbal inspiration, but at the same time confessed to the deepest reverence for the divine authority of the Holy Scriptures.* Says Lichtenberg: "Without admitting either the infallibility of the canon or the plenary inspiration of the text, and while reserving the right to submit both to the test of historical criticism, the School of Conciliation does not the less proclaim the authority of the Bible in matters of religion" (*History of German Theology in the Nineteenth Century, p.* 470).

(2) *The School of Hengstenberg.* Naturally, the mediating character of the preceding school was also its weakness. It did not serve to check the course of Rationalism. A far more effective reaction appeared in the school of *Hengsten-*

berg, who returned to the principles of the Reformation. He *believed in the plenary inspiration of the Bible, and consequently defended its absolute infallibility.* He took his stand squarely on the Confessional Standards of the Lutheran Church. It is true that he was somewhat violent in his polemics, rather dogmatic in his assertions, and that he occasionally reveals a tendency to allegorize rather freely. But, on the whole, his exegetical work gives evidence of profound philological and historical erudition, and of believing insight into the truth of divine revelation. Among his disciples and followers we find K. F. Keil, Hävernick and Kurtz.

c. *Attempts to go beyond the Grammatico-Historical sense.* The lasting result of this period is the establishment of the Grammatico-Historical method of interpretation. We find this represented in such Hermeneutical manuals as those of C. A. G. Keil, Davidson, P. Fairbairn, A. Immer, and M. S. Terry. But gradually a tendency is becoming apparent that is not quite satisfied with the Grammatico-Historical Interpretation, and therefore endeavors to supplement it.

(1) *Kant held that only the moral interpretation of the Bible had religious significance.* According to him, the ethical improvement of man must be the controlling principle in the exposition of the Word of God. Whatever does not answer to this purpose must be rejected.

(2) *Olshausen put in a plea for "the deeper sense of Scripture."* For him, this was not something apart from the literal sense, but something intimately connected with it, and even based on it. *The way to find the deeper sense is to recognize "the divine revelation in Scripture, and its central point, Christ, in their living unity with God as well as with humanity"* (Immer). This deeper sense is the kernel of God's revelation.

While pleading for it, Olshausen warns against the old allegorical interpretation. To a certain extent, R. Stier followed in his wake.

(3) *Germar espoused what he called the Pan-harmonic interpretation* of Scripture. *"He demands the thorough harmony of the meaning discovered in Scripture, insofar as it is to be regarded as a revelation of God, with the utterances of Christ and with all else which is true and certain"* (Reuss). This principle is, of course, true as far as it goes, but leaves room for subjective speculation as to the extent to which the Bible is to be recognized as a revelation of God, and as to the things that are true and certain.

(4) *T. Beck advanced the so-called pneumatic or spiritual interpretation.* He demanded the spirit of faith in the interpreter. This spirit, according to him, would give birth to the conviction that the various parts of Scripture form an organic whole. And *the separate parts of the Bible should be interpreted in the light of this general physiognomy,* as it reveals itself in those parts of Scripture whose meaning is not in doubt. This is practically equivalent to saying that Scripture must be interpreted according to the analogy of faith.

The search for some principle of interpretation that will serve to complement the Grammatico-Historical sense is also characteristic of the works of Lutz, Hofmann, Klausen, Landerer, and others. We confidently expect that the future will bring greater unanimity in this particular among those who accept the Bible as the inspired Word of God.

QUESTIONS: What is the difference between verbal and plenary inspiration? In what different forms is the theory of partial inspiration presented? Is it possible for an interpreter to be without prepossessions? Is the principle of accommodation recognized in the Bible; and if so, how? What serious objection is there to Semler's theory of accommodation? What is the main characteristic of Rationalism? Why are some German scholars called "mediating theologians"? Why is the Grammatico-Historical interpretation insufficient?

LITERATURE: Diestel, *Geschichte,* pp. 556-781; Farrar, *History,* pp. 397-437; Reuss, *History, II,* pp. 587-625; Gilbert, *Interpretation,* pp. 249-292; Immer, *Hermeneutics,* pp. 55-83; Elliott, *Hermeneutics,* pp. 29-34.

IV. The Proper Conception of the Bible, the Object of Hermeneutica Sacra

A logical treatment of *Hermeneutica Sacra* requires, first of all, a description of its object, *the Bible;* for special Hermeneutics must always adapt itself to the class of literature to which it is applied. The unique character of the Bible will also, to a certain extent, determine the principles that are to govern its interpretation. This does not mean, however, that all the qualities of the Bible must be described, but only that those characteristics should be elucidated that bear, in one way or another, on its interpretation.

A. The Inspiration of the Bible

In discussing the character of the Bible, it is but natural to assign the first place to that great and all-controlling principle of which our Confession says: "We confess that this Word of God was not sent nor delivered by the will of man, but that *holy men of God spake as they were moved by the Holy Ghost,* as the apostle Peter saith. And that afterwards God, from a special care which He has for us and our salvation, commanded his servants, the Prophets and Apostles, to commit his revealed Word to writing; and He himself wrote with his own finger the two tables of the law. Therefore we call such writings holy and divine Scriptures" (Art. III, *Confessio Belgica*).

The Bible is divinely inspired—that is the one great principle that controls Hermeneutica Sacra. It cannot be ignored with impunity. Any theory of interpretation that disregards it, is fundamentally deficient, and will not be conducive to our understanding of *the Bible as the Word of God.*

But the assertion that the Bible is inspired is not sufficiently definite. The meaning of the term "inspiration" is rather indefinite, and requires greater precision. *By inspiration we understand that supernatural influence exerted on the sacred writers by the Holy Spirit, by virtue of which their writings are given divine truthfulness, and constitute an infallible and sufficient rule of faith and practice.* It means, as Dr. Warfield expresses it, that the writers did not work on their own initiative, but "as moved by the divine initiative and borne by the irresistible power of the Spirit of God along ways of his choosing to ends of his appointment." And when it is said that the writers were guided by the Holy Spirit in writing the books of the Bible, the term "writing" must be taken in a comprehensive sense. It includes the investigation of documents, the collection of facts, the arrangement of material, the very choice of words, in fact all the processes that enter into the composition of a book. Inspiration must be distinguished from revelation in the restricted sense of immediate communication of God in words. The former secures infallibility in teaching, while the latter adds to the store of knowledge. But both of them must be regarded as modes of the revelation of God in the wider sense; modes, i.e., in which God makes known to man His will, His operations, and His purposes.

1. SCRIPTURAL PROOF FOR DIVINE INSPIRATION. Many interpreters are decidedly opposed to any such conception of divine inspiration. They often represent it as a theory devised by conservative theologians to make the Bible square with their preconceived notions of what the character of the Word of God ought to be. But it is a great mistake to regard the idea of divine inspiration as defined above, as a philosophical theory imposed upon the Bible. The outstanding fact is that it is a Scriptural doctrine, just as much as the doctrines of God and providence, of Christ and the atonement, and others. The

Bible offers us a large number of data for a doctrine of (i.e., respecting) Scripture. In the following paragraphs, the most important Biblical proofs for the divine inspiration of the Bible are briefly indicated.

a. *The Bible plainly teaches that the organs of revelation were inspired,* when they communicated orally to the people the revelations which they had received.

(1) *The expressions which the Bible employs to describe the prophetic state and function are such as to imply direct inspiration.* Nothing can be inferred from the name *nabi,* because it is of uncertain derivation. But the classical passage, Ex. 7:1, clearly teaches us that a prophet is one who speaks for God to man, or, more specifically, one who brings the words of God to man. Cf. also Deut. 18:18; Jer. 1:9; II Pet. 1:21. Moreover, we are told that the Spirit of God came or fell upon the prophets; that the hand of Jehovah was strong upon them; that they received the word of God, and were under constraint to utter it (Isa. 8:11; Jer. 15:17; Ezek. 1:3; 3:22; 37:1).

(2) *The prophetic formulae clearly show that the prophets were conscious of coming to the people with the word of the Lord.* In unburdening their souls, they were cognizant of the fact that God filled their minds with a content that did not originate in their own consciousness. Hence the following formulae: "Thus saith the Lord"; "Hear ye the word of the Lord"; "Thus hath the Lord God showed unto me"; "The word of the Lord came unto . . ."

(3) There is another remarkable feature in the prophetic writings that points in the same direction. In many of their discourses in which the Lord is introduced as speaking, *the prophets suddenly turn from the use of the third to that of the first person,* without any transitional "saith the Lord."

In other words, they surprise the reader by beginning to speak *as if they were God.* Cf. Isa. 3:4; 5:3 ff.; 10:5 ff.; 27:3; Jer. 5:7; 16:21; Hos. 6:4 ff.; Joel 2:25; Amos 5:21 ff.; Zech. 9:7; etc. This would be unexampled boldness on the part of the prophets, if they were not absolutely sure that God was putting the words, which they were speaking, into their mouths as His own.

(4) Turning to the New Testament, we find that Christ promised His disciples *the Holy Spirit, to teach them all things, and to bring to their remembrance whatsoever He had taught them* (John 14:26). This promise was fulfilled on the day of Pentecost, and, from that time on, the disciples speak as infallible teachers of the people. They know that their words are the words of God (I Thess. 2:13), and feel confident that their testimony is the testimony of God (I John 5:9-12).

b. *The Bible teaches the inspiration of the written word.*

The foregoing certainty creates a *presumption* in favor of the inspiration of the organs of revelation in writing the books of the Bible. If God deemed it necessary that they should bring their oral message to the people under the direction of the Holy Spirit, He can hardly have regarded it as less essential that their writings should be safe-guarded in the same way. But we need not rest satisfied with presumptive evidence. The Bible actually teaches the inspiration of the written Word. It is true that not a single passage can be quoted which asserts explicitly the inspiration of the whole Bible, but the evidence is cumulative and leaves no doubt on this point.

(1) In the days of the New Testament, the Jews possessed a collection of writings, technically designated *he graphe* (the Scripture), or *hai graphai* (the Scriptures) (Rom. 9:17; Luke 24:27). *The he graphe are repeatedly quoted in the New Testament as having divine authority.* For Christ and His

disciples, an appeal to *he graphe* was the end of all controversy. Their "it is written" was equivalent to, "God says." Moreover, these writings are sometimes designated in a way that points to their sacred character, for instance, they are called *graphai hagiai* (Rom. 1:2), and *ta hiera grammata* (II Tim. 3:15). And besides these, there is even a description that points directly to their divine character. They are called "the oracles of God" (Rom. 3:2). In the classical passage, II Tim. 3:16, it is perfectly clear that the Scriptures in their entirety, conceived as a direct divine revelation, are meant.

(2) *There are a number of quotations from the Old Testament in the New that identify God and Scripture as speakers.* A striking example is found in Heb. 1:5-13, where seven Old Testament words are quoted, and are said to have been spoken by God, viz., Ps. 2:7; II Sam. 7:14; Deut. 32:43 (LXX), or Ps. 97:7; Ps. 104:4; Ps. 45:6,7; Ps. 102:24-27; Ps. 110:1. In looking up these passages, we notice that in some of them God is, and in others, He is not the speaker. What Scripture says, is simply ascribed to God. Moreover, in Rom. 9:17 and Gal. 3:8, Old Testament words are quoted with the formula, "the Scripture saith" ("preached"), while in the passages cited, Ex. 9:16; Gen. 22:18, God is the speaker. *This identification was possible only on the basis of a strict view of inspiration.*

(3) *The locus classicus for the inspiration of the Bible is II Tim. 3:16.* For a detailed interpretation of this verse, we refer to the Commentaries. A few remarks must suffice here. In the immediately preceding context, the apostle speaks of the advantages of Timothy in that he had received a strictly religious education, and had also from childhood known the Holy Scriptures, i.e., the Old Testament. And now, in the 16th verse, the apostle emphasizes the great importance of these Scriptures. From this, it follows that *he graphe* also re-

fers to the Old Testament as a whole. The word *theo-pneustos* means *God-breathed,* i.e., the product of the creative breath of God. The Greek word *pasa* is rendered by some "all," and by others "every," which makes very little difference, since the one emphasizes the totality, and the other every part of it. Again, some render: "All (every) Scripture is given by inspiration of God, and is profitable," etc.; and others: "All (every) Scripture given by inspiration of God is also profitable," etc. But even this makes no great difference, *for the inspiration of the Old Testament is either asserted or implied.*

(4) *Another important passage is II Pet.* 1:19-21, where the apostle assures his readers that what had been made known to them of the power and coming of the Lord Jesus Christ, did not rest on cunningly devised fables, but on the word of eye-witnesses. And then he adds that they have even better testimony in the prophetic word (by which Dr. Warfield understands the whole Old Testament). This is called more sure, *because it is not of private interpretation, i.e., not the result of human investigation, nor the product of the writer's own thinking.* It came not by the will of man, but as a gift of God.

(5) *Still another passage of considerable importance is I Cor.* 2:7-13. Paul points to the fact that the wisdom of God, which was hidden from eternity, and which only the Spirit of God could know, had been revealed to him. And then he continues: "Which things we also teach, *not in the words which man's wisdom teacheth, but which the Holy Ghost teacheth.*" Since he uses the present tense, this applies also to the things which he was writing to the Corinthians.

c. *The Bible teaches that inspiration also extended to the words that were employed by the writers.* It is a well-known fact that many who profess to believe that the Bible is inspired are emphatic in their denial of verbal inspiration. They find satisfaction in the acceptance of some kind of partial inspiration, as, for instance, that only the thoughts and not the words, or that only the matters pertaining to faith and life, or, more limited still, that only the words of Jesus, were inspired. Some object to the term "verbal inspiration," because it is apt to suggest a mechanical theory of inspiration, and prefer to use the term "plenary inspiration." There is no objection to this, if it be understood to mean, among other things, that this supernatural guidance of the Holy Spirit extended to the very choice of the words, for this is certainly taught in the Bible, both by express statement and by implication. Notice especially the following:

(1) In the passage already referred to under b (4), Paul claims to teach the things that were revealed by the Spirit of God, "not in *words* which man's wisdom teacheth, but in *words* which the Holy Ghost teacheth." Here the apostle clearly refers to the individual words as words taught by the Holy Spirit, and the double expression adds strength to his statement.

(2) When the Lord calls Jeremiah to his difficult task, he says: "Behold, I have put my *words* in thy mouth." Since He exercised such special care as to the words in which Jeremiah brought his revelations to Israel, the presumption is that He exercised similar care with respect to the words in which the prophet gave those revelations a permanent form for all future generations.

(3) According to John 10:33, the Jews were offended, because as they said, Jesus was making himself God. In answering this charge, Jesus appeals to a word of Scripture, viz., Ps. 82:6, where judges are called *gods,* and at the same time points to the fact that Scripture cannot be annulled, but has incontestable authority. Since He bases his argument on the use of a single word, it is implied that every word has divine authority.

(4) In Gal. 3:16, Paul founds his whole argument on the use of a singular rather than a plural. This argument of the apostle has been attacked on the ground that the Hebrew word to which he refers cannot be used in the plural to denote posterity. Cf. Gen. 13:15. But this does not destroy the validity of his argument, for the writer of Genesis might have used another word or expression in the plural. And even if it did, the passage would still prove that Paul believed in the inspiration of the individual words.

2. Relation of the Divine and the Human in Scriptural Authorship. From the preceding, it is quite clear that a double factor, the divine and the human, operated in the production of the Bible; and now the question arises concerning how the two were related to each other in the composition of the books of the Bible. To put the question in a more concrete form: Were the human writers merely as a pen in the hand of God? Were they simply amanuenses, who wrote what God dictated? Was their own personality suppressed when the Spirit of God came upon them and directed them to write what He desired? Were their memory and imagination, understanding and judgment, desires and will inactive when they were moved by the Holy Spirit? To all such questions there can be but one answer in view of the data of Scripture.

a. *The human authors of the Bible were not mere machines, nor even amanuenses. The Holy Spirit did not abridge their freedom, nor destroy their individuality.* The following proofs seem decisive on this point:

(1) *In many cases, the authors investigated beforehand the matter of which they intended to write.* Luke tells us in the proem of his Gospel that he had done this; and the authors of the books of Kings and Chronicles repeatedly refer to their sources.

(2) *The writers often gave expression to their own experiences,* as Moses did in the opening and closing chapters of Deuteronomy, and Luke, in the last half of the Acts of the Apostles. The Psalmists sang of their personal sin and of the pardoning grace received; of the dangers that surrounded them and their wonderful deliverances.

(3) *Many of the biblical books have an occasional character.* Their composition was prompted by external circumstances, and their character determined by the moral condition and the religious status of the original readers. In the New Testament, this applies particularly to the Epistles of Paul, Peter, and Jude, but also, though in a lesser degree, to the other writings.

(4) *The various books are characterized by a striking difference in style.* Alongside of the exalted poetry of the Psalms and the Prophets, we have the common prose of the Historians. Side by side with the pure Hebrew of Isaiah, we have the Aramaising language of Daniel, the dialectical style of Paul, as well as the simple diction of John.

b. It is perfectly evident, therefore, that the Holy Spirit employed the writers of the Bible just as they were, and as He himself had prepared them for their task, with their personal idiosyncrasies, their character and temperament, their talents and education, their likes and dislikes, without suppressing their personality. *There is one important limitation, however. The Holy Spirit could not permit their sinful nature to express itself.*

From all that has been said, it follows that the Bible has a divine and human aspect. This is not equivalent to saying that it has alongside of the divine also a human element. We are not warranted in parcelling the Bible out and assigning portions of it to God and man respectively. The Bible is, in all its parts, both in substance and form, down to the least minutiae, a book that comes from God. At the same time, it was composed, from the beginning to the end, through the instrumentality of man, and bears all the marks of human authorship that are consistent with infallibility. We cannot fully understand the process of inspiration, though certain analogies may help us to realize its possibility. It is a mystery that defies explanation, and must be accepted by faith.

3. OBJECTIONS AGAINST THE DOCTRINE OF VERBAL INSPIRATION. Many objections have been raised against the doctrine of verbal or plenary inspiration; and we should never make light of them, but give them due consideration. Some of them have a great semblance of plausibility, such as those that are based on the so-called phenomena of Scripture, such as textual errors, seeming discrepancies, supposedly incorrect and misapplied quotations, dual representations, and doublets. These derive their strength from the supposed fact that a truly scientific theory of inspiration must be based on an inductive study of all those phenomena. But this means that man, instead of accepting the plain teachings of the Bible respecting its inspiration, wants to make out for himself how far the Scriptures are inspired; and this is essentially Rationalistic. We should accept the teaching of the Bible as final on this point, as on every other, and then seek to adjust the phenomena of Scripture to the biblical doctrine of inspiration. And if this seems impossible for the present, we should reveal our faith in waiting patiently for further light. Let us always remember the words of Dr. Warfield, that "it is a settled logical principle that so long as the proper evidence by which a proposition is established remains unrefuted all so-called objections brought against it pass out of the category of objections to its truth into the category of difficulties to be adjusted to it."

a. There is one point, however, that calls for brief consideration. *The assertions that the Scriptures are, in every particular, infallibly inspired, refer only to the autographa, and not, in the same sense, to the manuscripts now in our possession, the present editions of the Bible, and the translations.* The original autographa were penned under divine guidance, and were therefore absolutely infallible. But it is not claimed that a perpetual miracle preserved the sacred text from the errors of the copyists. A comparison of the manuscripts clearly reveals the presence of such errors. Now, some infer from this that the inspiration of the Bible has therefore after all very little significance, and does not insure the infallibility of the Scriptures as we possess them. But let us remember that the only conclusion that follows from the facts just mentioned is that, insofar as there are errors of transcription in the present Bible, we are without the Word of God.

The fact remains, however,—and this is very important—that, aside from the comparatively few and relatively insignificant errors, we are in possession of the verbally inspired Word of God. Just what this means may be best inferred from the words of Moses Stuart and Garbett (quoted by Patton), both of whom made a special study of the text of Scripture. Says the former: "Out of some eight hundred thousand various readings of the Bible that have been collected, about seven hundred and ninety-five thousand are of about as much importance to the sense of the Greek and Hebrew Scriptures as the question in English orthography is, whether the word *honour* shall be spelled with a *u* or without it. Of the remainder, some change the sense of particular passages or expressions, or omit particular words or phrases; but no one doctrine of religion is changed, not one precept is taken away, not one important fact is altered, by the whole of the various readings collectively taken." And the latter says: "Let every word affected by these variations be put on one side, not as certainly uninspired, but as not being certainly inspired, because it is not certainly identical with the original autographs. It will be quite enough if the verbal inspiration of all the rest be admitted. For this inspired portion, on which variation of reading has not thrown the shadow of a question, contains so entirely every expressive and emphatic word, that the denial of inspiration to the remainder becomes simply negatory, if it be not ridiculous" (Patton, *Inspiration of the Scriptures,* p. 113 f.). In the words of Dr. Patton: "According to our view, an infallible autograph has been perpetuated by the industry of transcribers, and has been changed only in some unimportant details through the mistakes of copyists" (p. 115).

b. Finally, there are many Hermeneutical writers and exegetes, who are decidedly opposed to the *a priori* of a divine inspiration in their exegetical labors. Immer advances the principle, "that *every presupposition which would in any way anticipate the exegetical result is inadmissible.*" And he contends that the *"unconditional belief in the authority and inspiration of Scripture"* is such a presupposition (Herm., pp. 92, 93). But:

(1) He himself points out in the sequel *that no interpreter can discard all presuppositions.* It would seem that he would have to set himself aside, which is impossible. He cannot relinquish his deepest convictions, nor assume an indifferent attitude towards the author whom he seeks to understand. *And certainly a Reformed theologian cannot divest himself of the firm conviction, which is not merely a matter of the mind but of the heart, that the Bible is the infallible Word of God.*

(2) *The presupposition that the Bible is the inspired Word of God* and therefore has divine authority, while it gives us the assurance that every part of it is true and that it cannot be self-contradictory, *does not, as a rule, determine our exegesis*

of particular passages one way or another. It leaves us great freedom of movement and freedom of choice.

(3) It is a remarkable fact that *they, who have such conscientious scruples against the presupposition of divine inspiration in their exegetical labors, are often controlled by prepossessions that determine the results of their interpretations to a far greater extent than the doctrine of inspiration would.* One of these prepossessions of the present day, productive of much evil and of the subversion of many a Scripture passage, is the theory of evolutionary development as applied to the religion of Israel.

QUESTIONS: Were the organs of revelation inspired only in writing the books of the Bible, or also in their oral teaching? How did the inspiration of the Prophets differ from that of the Apostles? What elements were included in graphical (Kuyper), or transcriptive (Cave) inspiration? How does the inspiration of the writers differ from that of their writings? What is the difference between the inspiration, say, of Shakespeare, and that of David? Was it essential that the inspiration should extend to the very words used? What objections are raised against this doctrine of inspiration?

LITERATURE: Lee, *The Inspiration of the Scripture;* Bannerman, *Inspiration of the Scriptures;* H. McIntosh, *Is Christ Infallible and is the Bible True?* Warfield, *Revelation and Inspiration;* Orr, *Revelation and Inspiration;* Patton, *Inspiration of the Scriptures;* Sanday, *Inspiration;* Ladd, *The Doctrine of Sacred Scripture,* 2 vols.; Daubanton, *De Theopneustie der Heilige Schrift;* Kuyper, *Hedendaagsche Schriftcritiek;* Bavinck, H., *Philosophy of Revelation;* Girardeau, *Discussions of Theological Questions;* Grosheide, *Nieuw-Testamentische Exegeze;* Honig, *Is de Bijbel op Bovennatuurlijke wijze Geinspireerd?* Berkouwer, *Het probleem der Schriftcritiek;* Calvinistic Conference Lectures, 1943, *The Word of God and the Reformed Faith;* Westminster Seminary Faculty, *The Infallible Word.*

B. Unity and Diversity in the Bible

1. THE VARIOUS BOOKS OF THE BIBLE CONSTITUTE AN OR-
GANIC UNITY. The word "organic" should be stressed. This
unity is not a mere mechanical one, consisting of different
parts that were prepared with a view to their mutual correla-
tion, like the parts of a watch, and that were finally collected
in one volume. The Bible is not to be compared to a cathedral,
constructed according to the plans and specifications of an
architect, but to a stately tree, the product of progressive
growth. The Bible was not made, but grew, and the composition of its several books marks the stages of its progressive
development. It is, in the last analysis, the product of a single
mind, the embodiment of a single fruitful principle, branch-
ing out in various directions. The different parts of it are
mutually dependent, and are all together subservient to the
organism as a whole. Scripture itself testifies to its unity in
more than one way. Notice particularly the following:

a. *The passages that were quoted to prove the inspiration of
the Bible, and many others that might be added to these, point
to the fact that it has one primary author.* It is in all its parts
the product of the Holy Spirit.

b. *The contents of the Bible, notwithstanding their variety,
reveal a wonderful unity.* All the books of the Bible have
their binding center in Jesus Christ. They all relate to the
work of redemption and to the founding of God's Kingdom
on earth. Moreover, they all agree in their doctrinal teaching
and in their practical bearing on life. It has been one of the
marvels of the ages that 66 books, which gradually came into existence in the course of 1600 years, should reveal such
remarkable unanimity.

c. *The progressive character of God's revelation is also an
effective proof of its unity.* The study of *Biblical Theology*

or *Historia Revelationis* is making this increasingly apparent. The Scriptures reveal the development of a single divine thought with several sub-divisions, viz., that of the grace of God in Jesus Christ for the redemption of sinners. They show us the bud of the divine promises gradually opening into a beautiful flower. The coming Christ casts his shadows before him, and finally appears in person.

d. *The collective quotations of Scripture also point to its unity.* New Testament writers often illustrate or support some particular truth by quoting from several Old Testament books, and thereby reveal their conviction that these are of equal divine authority. We find an example of this in Rom. 3:10-18, where Paul quotes Eccles. 7:20; Ps. 14:2,3; 5:10; 140:4; 10:7; Isa. 59:7,8; Ps. 36:2. For other examples, cf. Heb. 1:5-13; 2:6-8,12,13. In connection with the first, Turpie says: "This quotation, then, made up of these several passages, gives us an example of a *combined* quotation; and, as it is preceded by 'according as it is written,' makes known that the *different writings* from which they were taken—viz., Psalms, Ecclesiastes, and Isaiah—are *equally* Scripture, and stand on the *same* level. If their statements were of *different* values, why place them *all* together?" (*The New Testament View of the Old,* p. 33).

e. *More indirectly, the unity of Scripture is proved by the significant fact that the New Testament authors, in quoting from the Old Testament, occasionally alter the passages quoted somewhat, or apply them in a sense that is not apparent in the Old Testament.* This can hardly be defended, except on the presumption that the Holy Spirit is, in the last analysis, the author of the whole Bible, and naturally had the right to quote and apply his own words as He saw fit.

2. ALONGSIDE OF THIS UNITY, HOWEVER, THE BIBLE ALSO REVEALS THE GREATEST DIVERSITY. There are several distinc-

tions that should be borne in mind in the interpretation of Scripture.

a. *The distinction between the Old and New Testament.* These differ in the following particulars:

(1) *As to contents.* The Old Testament contains the promise; the New Testament, the fulfillment. The former points forward to the coming of Christ, and leads up to him; the latter takes in him its starting-point, and looks back upon his completed sacrifice as the atonement for the sin of the world. The Old Testament is the bud, the New Testament, the flower; or, as Augustine expressed it: "The New Testament lies hid in the Old, the Old lies open in the New."

(2) *As to form.* The Old Testament is prophetical, while the New is apostolical. The symbolical element, which is very prominent in the former, is reduced to a minimum in the latter. Moreover, the divine factor is far more prominent in the Old Testament than in the New. The human authors of many Old Testament books are not known, and in the Prophets they are often, as it were, submerged in the divine author. Moreover, the Holy Spirit acts upon them from without. In the New Testament, on the other hand, the Holy Spirit dwells in the Church, and operates on the apostles from within. The divine factor is largely lost to sight.

(3) *As to language.* The Old Testament is written in the Hebrew language, with the exception of some parts of Daniel and a few verses in Jeremiah and Ezra, while the New Testament is written in Hellenistic Greek.

b. *The distinction between the various books of the Bible.* The fact that the Holy Spirit employed prophets and apostles, with their personal idiosyncrasies, with their natural talents and their acquired knowledge, in an organic way, naturally gave rise to great diversity. Each author gave his book a

certain definite stamp. Each one developed his own thoughts
in a distinctive way, presented them as occasion demanded, and
expressed them in a characteristic style. There is a great difference, for instance, between Isaiah and Jeremiah, between
Paul and John. They do not all have the same vocabulary,
nor write the same style. Their writings do not have the same
historical setting, and do not present the truth from the same
point of view. Each book of the Bible has an individual character.

c. *The distinction between the fundamental forms of God's
revelation*:

(1) God embodied His revelation partly in the form of *historical narratives*. It is of the utmost importance to bear in
mind that the historical facts narrated in the Bible also form
an essential part of the divine revelation, and should be interpreted as such.

(2) Again, God made known his will in part, by means of
didactical writings or discourses. In the Old Testament, we
find these especially in the Law and in the Chokmah literature ·
while in the New Testament they are found in the parables
and discourses of the Saviour, and in the Epistles.

(3) Then, too, He has given us an insight into the mysteries of His council through *prophecy*. This interprets the ways
of God in the past, reveals His will for the present, and opens
up bright vistas in the future for the consolation of the people of God.

(4) Finally, He also revealed himself in *poetry,* in which
we listen to strains as of a mighty orchestra. Dr. Stuart Robinson says beautifully: "Notes from the stricken chords of
the heart of God lead the strain, and notes from all the strick-
en chords of the human soul answer in responsive chorus."

QUESTIONS: Is the Bible a planned book? If so, in what sense?

Why does it constitute an organic rather than a mechanical unity? What connecting links are there between the Old and the New Testaments? What accounts for the fact that in our day the diversity rather than the unity of the Bible is emphasized? Why should the interpretation proceed, first of all, on the assumption that the Bible is a unity? Why must it also take account of its diversity?

LITERATURE: J. Monroe Gibson, *The Unity and Symmetry of the Bible;* A. Saphir, *The Divine Unity of Scripture;* Grosheide, *De Eenheid der Nieuw-Testamentische Gods-openbaring;* Turpie, *The New Testament View of the Old;* Bernard, *The Progress of Doctrine.*

C. The Unity of the Sense of Scripture

It is of the greatest importance to understand at the outset that Scripture has but a single sense, and is therefore susceptible to a scientific and logical investigation. This fundamental principle must be placed emphatically in the foreground, in opposition to the tendency, revealed in history and persisting in some quarters even up to the present time, to accept a manifold sense,—a tendency that makes any science of Hermeneutics impossible, and opens wide the door for all kinds of arbitrary interpretations. The delusion respecting a multiple sense originated largely in a misunderstanding of some of the important features of Scripture, such as its figurative language, its mysterious and incomprehensible elements, its symbolical facts, rites and actions, its prophecies with a double or triple fulfilment, and its types of coming realities.

1. BASES FOR THIS PRINCIPLE. It must be maintained that Scripture, no matter how many significations the separate words may have, has but one proper sense. This follows necessarily from a consideration of the following:

a. *The veracity of God.* It is a settled principle among men that a man of undoubted veracity will habitually express himself in unequivocal language. The human conscience has never approved of the equivocation of the Jesuits. And if a

really truthful man would not consciously resort to the use
of ambiguous language, then certainly God, who is the absolute truth, cannot have given us a revelation that is calcula-
ted to mislead.

b. *The purpose of God's revelation.* God reveals His will
and the way of salvation to men, in order to glorify Himself
in the redemption of sinners. He had in mind a gracious and
glorious end. And in view of this, it is utterly inconceivable
that He should have provided man with a dubious revelation,
since this would defeat the very purpose which He sought to
realize.

c. *The necessary congruity between the revelation of the Lo-
gos in the mind of man and his revelation in nature and in
Scripture.* It is exactly the adaptation of the one to the other
that makes all knowledge possible. All revelation, in order to
be understood, must be rational. And it would be the height
of inconsistency to think that God had revealed himself in a
reasonable manner in nature, but not in Scripture, which is
said to constitute his most perfect revelation. It would mean
that the truth of the Bible could not be investigated by logical
methods, nor intellectually comprehended.

d. *The character of human language, in which the Bible is
written.* The logic of the human mind is naturally reflected
in the language that is used by man. And it is absolutely foreign to the character of this language that a word should have
two, three, or even more significations in the same connection.
If this were not so, all communication among men would be
utterly impossible.

2. SAFEGUARDS AGAINST MISUNDERSTANDING THIS PRIN-
CIPLE. But while we should constantly bear in mind the great
principle that Scripture has but one proper sense, we should
guard against several misunderstandings.

a. *It is necessary to distinguish between the real sense of a passage of Scripture and the sense ascribed to it by various interpreters.* The many interpretations often given to a single passage do not disprove the unity of the sense of Scripture.

b. *The distinction should also be borne in mind between the proper sense of a passage and the different ways in which it may be applied.* It may be turned to practical use according to circumstances, whether it be for warning or exhortation, encouragement or rebuke.

c. *Then, too, it is of great importance to discriminate between the literal and the mystical sense,* and to understand that they together do not constitute a double but only a single sense. Several passages of Scripture have, besides their literal, also a symbolical or typical meaning. The things mentioned are symbols or types of other things. In all such cases, the mystical sense is based on the literal, and constitutes the proper sense of the Word of God.

d. *Finally, a careful distinction must be made between a double fulfilment of prophecy and a double sense.* Some prophecies are fulfilled in several successive facts or events. In such cases, the earlier fulfilments are partial and typical of those yet to come. And it is only in the final complete fulfilment that the sense of those prophecies is exhausted. But this feature does not give us the right to speak of a double sense of prophecy.

If the question be asked, whether it is permissible to speak of *a deeper sense of Scripture (huponoia),* an affirmative answer may be given. But it is necessary to guard against misunderstanding. Properly understood, *the deeper sense of the Bible does not constitute a second sense.* It is in all cases based on the literal, and is the proper sense of Scripture. The real meaning of Scripture does not always lie on the surface.

There is no truth in the assertion that the intent of the secondary authors, determined by the grammatico-historical method, always exhausts the sense of Scripture, and represents in all its fulness the meaning of the Holy Spirit. Many of the Old Testament types pointed ultimately to New Testament realities; many prophecies found their final fulfilment in Jesus Christ, no matter how often they had obtained partial fulfilment; and many of the Psalms give utterance to the joy and sorrow, not merely of the poets, but of the people of God as a whole, and, in some cases, of the suffering and triumphant Messiah. These considerations lead us to what may be called, the deeper sense of Scripture.

QUESTIONS: How could the theory of a double or triple sense arise in connection with the figurative language of the Bible? In connection with types and symbols? In connection with prophecy? How do interpreters often encourage the idea of a double sense? What is the so-called "deeper sense" against which one must be on his guard?

LITERATURE: Elliott, *Hermeneutics*, pp. 35-50; Cunningham, *Theological Lectures*, Lect. 48.

D. The Style of Scripture: General Characteristics

The style of Scripture is discussed here only in a very general way, and from an exegetical rather than from a literary point of view. Only those general peculiarities are indicated that have some bearing on the interpretation of the Bible, and that are more or less unique.

1. THE SIMPLICITY OF THE STYLE OF SCRIPTURE. Both believing and unbelieving scholars often commented on the simplicity of the Bible. The most exalted subjects are treated there in a way that is at once profound and simple, the result of an immediate and perfect insight into the truth. The evident simplicity of style is characteristic of the Hebrew language, and, in

a measure, also of the Greek of the New Testament. Notice the following:

a. In the Hebrew language, nearly all roots consist of three radicals. There are only two tenses, the perfect and the imperfect; and but two genders, the masculine and the feminine. Compound verbs and nouns are few, and nearly all sentences are coordinate.

b. The relation between the different sentences is in many cases indicated by the simple copulative *vav* (and), where the logical connection would require a more specific conjunction. Hence this particle, though in itself only a general connective, may indicate several special relations. It may be *explicative* (even), Amos 3:11; 4:10; *adversative* (and yet, while yet), Judg. 16:15; Ps. 28:3; *inferential* (then, so then, therefore), Ezek. 8:32; *causal* (for, because), Ps. 5:12; *final* (in order that), chiefly with the cohortative and the jussive. In the New Testament *kai* is often used in much the same way.

c. The frequent occurrence of the *hendiadys*, in which two words connected by a conjunction express the same idea as a single word with a qualifier, e.g., "—and let them be for signs, and for seasons, and for days, and years" (Gen. 1:14); "—a city and a mother in Israel" (II Sam. 20:19); "—of the hope and resurrection of the dead I am called in question" (Acts 23:6).

d. Direct discourse is often found, where indirect discourse would be expected. Examples may be found in the following places: II Sam. 13:32; Isa. 3:6; Jer. 3:16; Ps. 2:3; Matt. 1:20, 23; 2:3, 5.(For some indication of the simplicity of the Greek of the New Testament, cf. under 5, below.)

2. THE LIVELINESS OF THE STYLE OF SCRIPTURE. Orientals are generally very vivid in their representations: and the authors of the Bible do not run counter to their character in this

respect. In several ways they lend color to the revelation of God that was mediated by them.

a. *They reveal a decided tendency to represent abstract truths in concrete forms.* Spiritual qualities are often described under the figure of those parts of the body by which they are symbolized. Thus, the might and anger of God are represented under the image of His arm and nose, respectively; and the expression of His benevolence or displeasure is associated with the lifting up or the hiding of His countenance. Cf. Ps. 89:13; 18:8; 4:6; 44:24. Probably sin is occasionally represented as personified in the sinner.

b. *They see nature round about them as instinct with life, and consequently personify it repeatedly.* All inanimate things are represented as either male or female, the particular gender depending on the qualities revealed. Intellect and will, emotions and desires, are ascribed to the whole creation. Examples of such an animated description of nature are found in Ps. 19:2,3; 96:12; 98:8; Isa. 55:12; and Rom. 8:19-22.

c. *The historians of the Bible do not simply narrate, but picture history.* They let the facts pass before the eyes of the readers as in a panorama. Hence the frequent use of the word "behold!" In all probability this also accounts for the use of the Hebrew imperfect with a *vav conversive* in continued narratives that begin with a perfect. The Oriental preferred to represent actions, not as completed in the past but as in the process of being completed, and therefore as continuing in the present. In the New Testament, something similar is found in the extensive use of the present.

d. *Certain redundant expressions also add to the liveliness of the style of Scripture,* as for instance: "he opened his mouth and spoke"; "he lifted up his eyes and saw"; "she lifted up her voice and wept"; "incline thine ear and hear."

3. THE EXTENSIVE USE OF FIGURATIVE LANGUAGE. This finds its explanation partly in the inability to describe spiritual and heavenly things in literal language, partly in the Oriental's perference for plastic and pictorial representation, and partly in a desire for variety and literary beauty. Since it will be necessary to discuss the figurative language of the Bible and its interpretation separately, we pass it by for the present.

4. THE PECULIAR PARALLELISM OF SENTENCES THAT CHARACTERIZES A GREAT DEAL OF THE BIBLICAL POETRY AND A PART OF ITS PROSE. Bishop Lowth was the first to use the term *parallelismus membrorum* to describe the peculiar feature that "in two lines or members of the same period, things for the most part answer to things, and words to words." It is found particularly in the Psalms and in the other poetical books of the Bible, but also in some of its prose writings. Bishop Lowth distinguished three kinds of parallelism, to which Jebb added a fourth. They are the following:

a. *Synonymous parallelism,* in which the same idea is repeated in different words. There may be mere *similarity* (*Ps.* 24:2; Job 6:5); or *identity* (Prov. 6:2; Ps. 93:3).

b. *Antithetic parallelism,* in which the second member of a line or verse gives the obverse side of the same thought. This is found especially in the book of Proverbs. It may be either *simple* (Prov. 14:34, Ps. 30:6); or *compound* (Isa. 1:3,19, 20).

c. *Synthetic parallelism,* also called constructive and epithetic. In it the second member adds something new to the first, or explains it. This may be either *correspondent,* when the first line corresponds with the third, and the second with the fourth (Ps. 27:1; 35:26,27); or *cumulative,* with a cumulation of successive ideas, sometimes leading up to a climax (Ps. 1:1,2; Isa. 55:6,7; Heb. 3:17).

d. *Introverted or chiastic parallelism,* defined as parallelism in reverse order, in which the hemistichs of the members are chiastically arranged (Prov. 23:15,16; 10:4,5; 13:24).

5. CHARACTERISTIC FEATURES OF NEW TESTAMENT LANGUAGE. Finally, the language of the New Testament has certain characteristic features. It is not the pure Greek of the classical period, but Hellenistic Greek, often called the *koine,* or common language. For a long time the position was maintained that the language of the New Testament was strongly influenced by the Greek of the Septuagint, and through it, by the Hebrew or Aramaic. The correctness of this position was called in question by such scholars as Deissmann, Moulton and Milligan, Robertson, and Goodspeed. Under their influence the opinion prevailed for a while that the Greek of the New Testament contains scarcely any real Hebraisms. Today, however, the pendulum is swinging somewhat in the other direction again. Due to the investigations of C. C. Torrey and his school, the earlier view, which recognized a rather strong influence of Aramaic on the *koine* of the New Testament, is once more gaining adherents. The issue has not yet been definitely settled, and therefore one can hardly speak with assurance as to the relative importance of various factors in shaping the language of the New Testament.

QUESTIONS: How does the style of the historical differ from that of the prophetical and poetical books? What characteristic differences are there between the style of Mark and Luke? Why is the style of John called Hebraistic? What characteristic contrasts are there in the writings of John? Which, in the Epistles of Paul?

LITERATURE: Girdlestone, *Foundations of the Bible,* pp. 89-98; Hastings, *Dictionary of the Bible,* and the *International Standard Bible Encyclopaedia,* Articles, "Language of the Old Testament"; and "Language of the New Testament"; Simcox, *The Writers of the New Testament;* Davidson, *Old Testament Prophecy,* pp. 159-192; Girdlestone, *The Grammar of Prophecy;* Immer. *Herme-*

neutics, pp. 125-144; Deissmann, *Light from the Ancient East;* Ibid., *Biblical Studies.*

E. The Exegetical Standpoint of the Interpreter—The Relation of the Interpreter to the Object of His Study

In distinction from the Church of Rome, *the Churches of the Reformation accepted the important principle that every individual has the right to investigate and to interpret the Word of God for himself.* It is true, they also held that the Church, in virtue of her *potestas doctrinae,* was entrusted with the important task of preserving, interpreting, and defending the Word of God, and was qualified for this paramount duty by the Holy Spirit. But they repudiated the idea that any ecclesiastical interpretation is *per se* infallible and binding on the conscience. The interpretations of the Church have divine authority only insofar as they are in harmony with the teachings of the Bible as a whole. And every individual must judge of this for himself. Protestants deny that God ever constituted the Church, in her appointed organs, as the special interpreter of the divine Word, and maintain the prerogative of every Christian to study and interpret Scripture. They base their position (1) on such passages as Deut. 13:1-3; John 5:39 (if the verb be indicative); and Gal. 1:8, 9; (2) from the fact that God holds every man responsible for his faith and conduct; and (3) from the additional fact that the Scriptures do not address themselves exclusively, nor even primarily, to the office-bearers in the Church, but to the people that constitute the Church of God.

This principle also implies that the attitude of the interpreter to the object of his study must be one of perfect freedom. The Church of Rome restricted this freedom successively (1) by an ecclesiastical translation; (2) by tradition, especially in the form of the *consensus omnium patrum;* (3) by the decisions of the councils; and (4) by the infallible dicta of the pope. Protestants never accepted such a theory in principle, though in practice they occasionally revealed a tendency to let Dogmatics or Confessional Standards lord it over the interpretation of the Bible. It goes without saying that every interpreter ought to take account of the exegetical labors of former ages that crystallized in the creeds, and should not lightly depart from what became a *communis opinio*. But he may never permit that which is the fruit of exegesis to become its norm. He cannot, consistently and legitimately, allow the Church to dominate in matters of interpretation.

But though it be true that *the interpreter* must be perfectly free in his labors, he *should not confuse his freedom with licentiousness*. He is indeed, free from all external restrictions and authority, but he is not free from the laws inherent in the object of his interpretation. In all his expositions he is bound by that which is written, and *has no right to ascribe his thoughts to the authors*. This principle is generally recognized today. It is quite different, however, when the position is maintained that *the freedom of the interpreter is also limited by the fact that the Bible is the inspired, and therefore self-consistent, Word of God*. And yet this principle must be honored by all Reformed interpreters.

QUESTIONS: Who was the first to defend the right of private judgment? How did the Reformers propose to settle differences of interpretation? Has the interpreter, who subscribed to a certain creed, the right to deviate from it in his expositions? To what measures should he resort in case of a conflict between his interpretation of the Bible and the creed?

LITERATURE: Bavinck, *Dogmatiek* I, p. 510 vv.; IV., pp. 456-460; Kuyper, *Encyclopaedie III*, p. 114 vv.; Cunningham, *Theological Lectures,* Lect. 47, 48; Muenscher, *Manual of Biblical Interpretation,* chap. 4.

V. Grammatical Interpretation

A. Meaning of the Separate Words

The Bible was written in human language, and consequently must be interpreted grammatically first of all. In the study of the text the interpreter can proceed in a twofold way. He can begin with the sentence, with the expression of the writer's thought as a unity, and then descend to particulars, to the interpretation of the separate words and concepts; or he can begin with the latter, and then gradually ascend to a consideration of the sentence, of the thought as a whole. From a purely logical and psychological point of view, the first method deserves preference. Cf. Woltjer, *Het Woord, zijn Oorsprong en Uitlegging,* p. 59. But for practical reasons it is generally advisable to begin the interpretation of foreign literature with a study of the separate words. Hence we shall follow this order in our discussion. Three things call for consideration here.

1. THE ETYMOLOGY OF THE WORDS. The etymological meaning of the words deserves attention first, not as being the most important for the exegete, but because it logically precedes all other meanings. As a rule it is not advisable that the interpreter should indulge very much in etymological investigations. This work is extremely difficult, and can, ordinarily, best be left to the specialists. Moreover, the etymological meaning of a word does not always shed light on its current signification. At the same time, it is advisable that the expositor of Scripture take notice of the *established* etymology of a word, since it may help to determine its real mean-

ing and may illumine it in a surprising manner. Think of the Hebrew words *kopher, kippurim*, and *kapporeth*, which are translated respectively "ransom," "redemptions" or "atonements," and "Mercy-seat." They are all derived from the root *kaphar*, which means "to cover," and contains the idea of a redemption or atonement brought about by a certain covering. Sin or the sinner is covered by the atoning blood of Christ, which was typified by the blood of the Old Testament sacrifices. Or, take the New Testament word *ekklesia*, derived from *ek* and *kalein*. It is a designation of the Church, both in the Septuagint and in the New Testament, and points to the fact that this consists of a people that is "called out," i.e., out of the world in special devotion to God.

EXERCISE: Find the original meaning of the following:
      a. Hebrew words: *chata', avah, tsaddiq, qahal, 'edhah;*
      b. Greek words: *kleronomia, makrothumia, eutrapelia, spermologos.*

2. THE CURRENT USE OF THE WORDS. The current signification of a word is of far more importance for the interpreter than its etymological meaning. In order to interpret the Bible correctly, he must be acquainted with the significations which the words acquired in the course of time, and with the sense in which the Biblical authors use them. This is the important point to be settled. Now it may be thought that this is easily done by consulting some good Lexicon, which generally gives both the original and the derivative meanings of the words, and generally designates in what sense they are employed in particular passages. And in most cases this is perfectly true. At the same time it is necessary to bear in mind that the Lexicons are not absolutely reliable, and that they are least so, when they descend to particulars. They merely embody those results of the exegetical labors of various interpreters that commended themselves to the discrimin-

ating judgment of the lexicographer, and often reveal a difference of opinion. It is quite possible, and in some cases perfectly evident, that the choice of a meaning was determined by dogmatical bias. Tregelles warns against this danger in the introductory word to the second edition of his Gesenius. Says he: "Hence arises the peculiar importance mentioned above, of properly attending to Hebrew philology. A real acquaintance with that language, or even the ability of properly using the works of competent writers, will often show that the dogmatic assertion that something very peculiar *must* be the meaning of a Hebrew word or sentence, is only a *petitio principii* devised for the sake of certain deductions which are intended to be drawn. It may be seen by any competent scholar, not only that such strange signification is not necessary, but also that it is often inadmissible, unless we are allowed to resort to the most arbitrary conjectures . . . The mode in which some have introduced difficulties into the department of Hebrew philology, has been by assigning new and strange meanings to Hebrew words, by affirming that such meanings *must* be right in particular passages (although nowhere else), and by limiting the sense of a root or a term, so as to imply that some incorrectness of statement is found on the part of the Sacred writers."

If the interpreter has any reason to doubt the meaning of a word, as given by the Lexicon, he will have to investigate for himself. Such labors are undoubtedly very fruitful, but they are also extremely difficult. (a) Most words have several meanings, some literal and some figurative, (b) The comparative study of analogous words in other languages requires careful discrimination, and does not always help us to fix the exact meaning of a word, since corresponding words in different languages do not always have exactly the same original and derivative meanings. (c) In the study of New Testament words, it is imperative that account should be taken, not only of the written, but also of the spoken *koine*. (d) It is not always safe to conclude from the meaning of a word in classical Greek its signification in the New Testament, since Christianity has in many cases given the words a new content. Moreover, it is precarious to assume that a word always has the same meaning in the Word of God. The revealing God spoke "at sundry times and in divers manners"; His revelation was progressive, and may have enriched the meaning of the words in the course of its development.

But, however difficult the task may be, this may not deter the interpreter. If necessary, he must make a thorough study of a word for himself. And the only way in which he can do it is by the inductive method. It will be incumbent on him (a) to ascertain, by the aid of Hebrew and Greek concordances, where the word is found; (b) to determine the meaning of the word in each one of the connections in which it occurs; and (c) to do this by means of internal rather than external helps. In the pursuance of such a study, the various significations of a word will gradually become apparent. The interpreter must beware, however, of hasty conclusions, and should never base his induction on only a part of the data at hand. Such inductive study may enable him (a) to determine whether a certain meaning, confidently ascribed to a word by the Lexicon, is indeed correct or (b) to obtain certainty respecting a signification that was represented as doubtful in the Lexicon; or (c) to discover a meaning that had never been ascribed to the word before.

The so-called *hapax legomena* constitute a special difficulty. These may be of two kinds, viz., (a) *absolute,* when a word is found but once in the whole range of known literature; and (b) *relative,* when there is only a single instance of its use in the Bible. The former are particularly perplexing for the interpreter. The origin of such words is often lost in obscurity, and their meaning can only be determined approximately, by means of the context in which they occur, and by the analogy of related words in the same or in other languages. Think of *epiousios* in Matt. 6:11; Luke 11:3; and of *pistikos* in Mark 14:3; John 12:3.

3. THE SYNONYMOUS USE OF WORDS. Every language contains both antonyms and synonyms. Synonymous words are those that have the same meaning, or agree in one or more of their meanings, though they may differ in others. They often agree in their fundamental signification, but give expression to different shades of it. The use of synonyms ministers to the beauty of a language insofar as it enables an author to vary his expressions. Moreover, it enriches a language by making it capable of expressing more minutely the different shades and aspects of any particular idea.

The languages in which the Bible was written are also rich in synonyms and synonymous expressions. It is to be regretted that these were not retained in the translations to a greater extent. In some cases this was quite impossible, but in others it might have been done. But even though some of the finer distinctions were lost in translation, the interpreter may never lose sight of them. He must have an open eye for all the related ideas of the Bible, and be quick to notice what they have in common and wherein they differ. This is the *sine qua non* of a discriminating knowledge of the Biblical revelation.

Here, again, external helps may be employed, such as Girdlestone's *Old Testament Synonyms,* Kennedy's *Hebrew Synonyms,* Trench's *New Testament Synonyms,* and Cremer's *Biblisch-Theologisches Wörterbuch.* But these works are not exhaustive, and the possibility exists that their distinctions do not commend themselves to the interpreter. In such cases, he will have to make an inductive study for himself which is extremely difficult. In the Preface to the eighth edition of his work, Trench gives some valuable hints for the proper conduct of such an investigation.

The importance of noting carefully the exact meaning of synonymous words may be illustrated by a few examples. In Isa. 53:2, three words are used to express the absence of external glory in the life of the Servant of the Lord. We read there: "He hath no form nor comeliness; and when we see him, there is no *beauty* that we should desire him." (Am. Rev.) The first word (*tho'ar*) means form," with the added idea of beauty, and therefore refers to a beautiful bodily form. Comp. I Sam. 16:18. The second (*hadar*) designates an ornament, and, as applied to God, is descriptive of majesty. It refers to the way in which the Lord appeared among men rather than to his physical form. He manifested himself in a state of humiliation. And the third (*mar'eh*, from *ra'ah*, "to see"), sometimes refers to an external appearance which is the expression of and therefore in harmony with an inner essential being. The meaning of the prophet seems to be that the external appearance of the Lord was not such as the Jews expected of the Messiah.

The New Testament furnishes a beautiful example in John 21:15-17. When the risen Lord inquired into the love of fallen Peter, He employed two words, viz., *agapao and phileo*. The distinction between the two is given by Trench in the following words: "The first expresses a more reasoning attachment of choice and selection, from a seeing in the object upon which it is bestowed that which is worthy of regard; or else from a sense that such is due toward the person so regarded, as being a benefactor, or the like; while the second, without being necessarily an unreasoning attachment, does yet give less account of itself to itself; is more instinctive, is more of the feelings or natural affections, implies more passion." The former, based upon admiration and respect, is a love that is controlled by the will and of an enduring character; while the latter, based on affection, is a love that is more impulsive and apt to lose its fervor. Now, when the Lord first puts the question to Peter, "lovest thou me?" he used the first word, *aqapao*. But Peter did not dare to answer affirmatively to the question, whether he loved the Lord with a permanent love that achieves its greatest triumphs in moments of temptation. So in answering, he employs the second word, *phileo*. The Lord repeats the question, and Peter again gives answer in the same way. Then the Saviour descends to the level of Peter, and in his third question uses the second word, as if He doubted even the *philein* of Peter. No wonder that the latter became sorrowful, and made an appeal to the omniscience of the Lord.

These examples suffice to prove the great importance of the study of synonyms. An interesting field of study opens up for the interpreter here. But just because this study is so fascinating, it may also become dangerous. Synonymous words always have a general, as well as a special distinctive signification; and the expositor should not proceed on the principle that, whenever such words are employed, their distinctive meaning should always be emphasized, for, if he does, he is liable to find himself entangled in all kinds of fanciful interpretations. The context in which a word is used, the predicates ascribed to it, and the adjuncts added to it, must determine whether a word is to be understood in a general or in a special sense. *If two or more synonymous words or expressions are found in the same passage, it is generally safe to assume that their special signification requires attention.*

EXERCISE: Study the following synonyms:

a. Old Testament: *'edhah and qahal,* Lev. 4:13; *chatta'th, 'avon,* and *pesha',* Ps. 32:5; *del* and *'ebhyon,* Prov. 14:31; *gebher* and *'adham,* Jer. 17:5.

b. New Testament: *de-esis, proseuche,* and *eucharistia,* I Tim. 2:1; *charis* and *eleos,* II Tim. 1:2; *sophia* and *phronesis,* Eph. 1:8; *morphe* and *schema,* Phil. 2:7; *mochthos* and *kopos,* I Thess. 2:9.

LITERATURE: Fairbairn, *Hermeneutical Manual,* pp. 79-106; Terry, *Biblical Hermeneutics,* pp. 73-100; Dalman, *The Words of Jesus;* Deissmann, *Biblical Studies;* Girdlestone, *Old Testament Synonyms;* Kennedy, *Hebrew Synonyms;* Trench, *New Testament Synonyms;* Cremer, *Biblisch-Theologisches Wörterbuch;* the various Concordances and Lexicons.

B. The Meaning of the Words in their Connection—*Usus Loquendi*

In the study of the separate words, the most important question is not that of their etymological meaning, nor even that of the various significations which they gradually acquired. The essential point is that of their particular sense in the connection in which they occur. The interpreter must determine whether the words are used in their general or in one of their special significations, whether they are employed in a literal or in a figurative sense. The discussion of the figurative use of words is left for a following paragraph. In the study of the words in their connection, the interpreter should proceed on the following principles:

1. "THE LANGUAGE OF SCRIPTURE SHOULD BE INTERPRETED ACCORDING TO ITS GRAMMATICAL IMPORT; AND THE SENSE OF ANY EXPRESSION, PROPOSITION, OR DECLARATION, IS TO BE DETERMINED BY THE WORDS EMPLOYED" (Muenscher, *Manual of Biblical Interpretation,* p. 107). In the last analysis, our theology finds its solid foundation only in the grammatical sense of Scripture. Theological knowledge will be faulty in proportion to its deviation from the plain meaning of the Bible. Though this canon is perfectly obvious, it is repeatedly violated by those who bring their preconceived ideas to bear upon the interpretation of the Bible. By means of forced exegesis, they attempt to make the

sense of Scripture square with their pet theories or opinions. Rationalists act in defiance of it, when they resolve the story of the fall into a myth; and Millenarians, when they find in I Thess. 4:16 proof for a twofold resurrection. The interpreter should carefully guard against this mistake, and conscientiously abide by the plain meaning of the words.

2. A Word Can Have But One Fixed Meaning in the Connection in Which it Occurs. This may seem so evident as to require no special mention. But experience teaches us that it is not superfluous to call attention to it. The desire to seem original and profound, and to surprise the common people by fanciful expositions of which they have never heard, sometimes tempts interpreters to lose sight of this simple canon of interpretation. It frequently happens that all the significations which a word in the abstract has, are ascribed to it in whatever connection it may occur. Such a mode of procedure must be condemned as being purely arbitrary. Its danger and folly may be illustrated by a few examples.

The Greek word *sarks* may designate (a) the solid part of the body, except the bones (I Cor. 15:39; Luke 24:39); (b) the whole substance of the body, when it is synonymous with *soma* (Acts 2:26; Eph. 2:15; 5:29); (c) the animal (sensuous) nature of man (John 1:13; Rom. 10:18); and (d) human nature as dominated by sin, the seat and vehicle of sinful desires (Rom. 7:25; 8:4-9; Gal. 5:16, 17). If an interpreter ascribed all these meanings to the word as it is found in John 6:53, he would thereby also attribute sin in an ethical sense to Christ, whom the Bible represents as the sinless one.

The Hebrew word *nakar* means (a) not to know, to be ignorant; (b) to contemplate, to look at anything as strange, or little known; and (c) to know, to be acquainted with. The first and third meanings are opposites. Hence it is perfectly obvious that, if an expositor should seek to combine these various meanings in the interpretation of a single passage like Gen. 42:8, the contrast which this verse contains would be lost, and pure nonsense would be the result.

This method of interpretation was fostered by Coccejus, who advocated the principle that all the possible meanings of a word in the Scriptures are to be united; but the interpreter must beware of this arbitrary method of procedure.

3. CASES IN WHICH SEVERAL MEANINGS OF A WORD ARE UNITED IN SUCH A MANNER THAT THEY ARE RESOLVED INTO A HIGHER UNITY DO NOT CONFLICT WITH THE PRECEDING CANON.

a. *Sometimes a word is used in its most general sense, so as to include its special meanings, though these are not emphasized.* When Jesus says to the disciples in John 20:21: "Peace be unto you," He means peace in the most comprehensive sense—peace with God, peace of conscience, peace among themselves, etc. And when Isaiah says in 53:4; "Surely, He hath borne our griefs" (literally: sicknesses), he certainly refers to the spiritual diseases of which the Servant of the Lord delivers his people. But in Matt. 8:17; we are told that this word was fulfilled in the Saviour's ministry of healing. The word of Isaiah is, therefore, taken to mean not only that the Servant of the Lord delivered his people from spiritual ills, i.e., from sin, but also from the resulting physical ailments.

b. *There are also cases in which one special meaning of a word includes another, which does not conflict with the purpose and connection of the passage in which it is found.* Under such circumstances, it is perfectly legitimate to unite the two. When John the Baptist says "Behold the Lamb of God that *taketh away* the sin of the world," he employs a word (*airo*) that means (1) to take up; and (2) to carry away. In this passage, the latter meaning clearly predominates, but it naturally includes the other. Jesus could not bear sin away without taking it upon himself.

c. *Then again, an author occasionally employs a word in a pregnant sense, so as to indicate far more than it really expresses.* This is done especially in the synecdoche, when a part is put for the whole. When the Saviour teaches his disciples to pray: "Give us this day our daily bread," the word "bread" undoubtedly stands for the necessaries of life in general. And when the Law says: "Thou shalt not kill," it forbids, according to the interpretation of Jesus, not merely murder, but anger, hatred and implacability as well.

The interpreter should be careful, however, not to combine various meanings of a word arbitrarily. He may encounter cases in which two or more significations of a word apparently fit the connection equally well, and be tempted to take the easy road of combining them. But this is not good exegesis. Muenscher holds that, in such cases, the meaning that exhibits the most full and fertile sense is to be preferred. It is better, however, to suspend judgment, until further study warrants a definite choice.

4. IF A WORD IS USED IN THE SAME CONNECTION MORE THAN ONCE, THE NATURAL ASSUMPTION IS THAT IT HAS THE SAME MEANING THROUGHOUT. Ordinarily an author will not use a word in two or three different senses in a single passage. This would, under ordinary circumstances, lead to confusion. Yet there are a few exceptions to the rule. In a few passages a word is repeated with a change of meaning. But these cases are of such a kind that the danger of misunderstanding is obviated. The character of the expression of the context makes it sufficiently clear that the word does not have the same sense in both cases. The following examples will suffice to illustrate this: Matt. 8:22, "Let the dead bury their dead"; Rom. 9:6, "For they are not all Israel that are of Israel"; II Cor.

5:21, "For He hath made him to be sin for us, who knew no sin, that we might be made the righteousness of God in him."

C. Internal Helps for the Explanation of Words

The question naturally arises, concerning how an interpreter can best discover what a word means in a certain connection. It may be thought that the most effective way is to consult a standard Lexicon, or some good Commentaries. And in many cases, this may be quite sufficient, but in others it may prove necessary for an expositor to judge for himself. Whenever this is the case, he shall have to resort to the use of internal helps. The following are the most important:

1. DEFINITIONS OR EXPLANATIONS WHICH THE AUTHORS THEMSELVES GIVE OF THEIR WORDS CONSTITUTE ONE OF THE MOST EFFICIENT HELPS. No one knows better than the author what particular sense he attaches to a word. The following examples may serve to illustrate what is meant: Gen. 24:2: "And Abraham said to *the eldest servant of his house,*" to which is added by way of definition, "that ruled over all that he had." II Tim. 3:17: "That the man of God may *be perfect,*" which is said to mean, "thoroughly furnished unto all good works." Heb. 5:14: "But strong meat belongeth to them that are of full age" (or, perfect), which is explained by the following words: "even those who by reason of use have their senses exercised to discern both good and evil."

2. THE SUBJECT AND PREDICATE OF A PROPOSITION MUTUALLY EXPLAIN EACH OTHER. In Matt. 5:13, where we read: "If the salt have lost its savour," the meaning of the verb *moranthei,* which may also signify, *to become foolish* (cf. Rom. 1:22), is determined by the subject, *salt.* In Rom. 8:19-23, the meaning of the subject, *creature,* is limited by the various predicates. The good angels are excluded by verse 20; the bad, by verses 19-21. The same verses make it impossible to include the wicked among men, while the 23rd verse also ex-

cludes the children of God. The idea is limited, therefore, to the irrational and inanimate creation.

3. PARALLELISM MAY AID IN DETERMINING THE MEANING OF A WORD. This applies especially to synonymous and antithetical parallelism. In Ps. 7:13 we read: "He hath also prepared for him *the instruments of death*," which is explained by the following member: "He ordaineth his arrows against the persecutors." In Isa. 46:11, the Lord says of himself that He is "calling a ravenous bird from the East," and this finds its explanation in the parallelism: "the man that executeth my counsel from a far country." Again, in II Tim. 2:13, Paul affirms respecting God that "He *abideth faithful*. He cannot *deny himself.*" The first expression explains the second, which in Luke 9:23 means to sacrifice personal interests and pleasures. In Prov. 8:35, we read: "For *whoso findeth me* findeth life"; and in the antithetical member of the parallelism in the following verse: "But he *that sinneth against me* wrongeth his own soul." The first explains the second, and clearly shows that the verb *chata'* is here used in its original sense, viz., to miss the mark. We might read therefore: "But he that misses me . . ."

4. PARALLEL PASSAGES ALSO CONSTITUTE AN IMPORTANT HELP. These are divided into two classes, viz., *verbal* and *real.* "When the same word occurs in similar connections, or in reference to the same general subject, the parallel is called verbal . . . Real parallels are those similar passages in which the likeness or identity consists, not in words or phrases, but in facts, subjects, sentiments or doctrines" (Terry, *Biblical Hermeneutics,* p. 121). Verbal parallels establish points of linguistic usage, while real parallels serve to explain points of historical, ethical, or dogmatical interest. For the present, we are concerned only with verbal parallels, which may serve to explain an obscure or unknown word. It is possible that

neither the etymology of a word, nor the connection in which it is found, are sufficient to determine its exact meaning. In such cases, it is of paramount significance to study parallel passages, in which the same word is found in a similar connection, or in reference to the same general subject. Each passage consulted must, of course, be studied in its connection.

In employing the aid of parallel passages, the interpreter must be sure that they are really parallel. In the words of Davidson. "It is not enough that the same term or phrase be found in both; there must be similarity of sentiment." For instance, Jonah 4:10 and I Thess. 5:5 are not parallel, though the expression "son(s) of a (the) night" is found in both. Neither are Prov. 22:2 and 29:13, though they are often regarded as such. Cf. Terry, *Biblical Hermeneutics,* p. 121. Moreover, it is necessary that the phrase or expression that calls for explanation be clearer in one passage than it is in the other, for it is impossible to explain an obscure passage by one that is equally dark. It is hardly necessary to remark in this connection that the interpreter should carefully guard against the mistake of trying to illustrate a perfectly clear passage by one that is less perspicuous. This policy is often followed by those who are interested in escaping the force of the positive teachings of the Bible. Furthermore, while parallel passages may be adduced from any part of Scripture, it is desirable to observe a certain order. The interpreter should seek for parallels, first of all, in the writings of the same author, since, as Davidson remarks, "the same peculiarities of conception and modes of expression are liable to return in different works proceeding from one person." Then the works of contemporaries should be consulted before those of others. Again, common sense dictates that writings of the same class have the priority over those that belong to different classes.

In illustrating the use of parallel passages, we distinguish between those that are properly, and those that are improperly so called.

a. *Parallels of words properly so called.* In Col. 1:16 we read: "For by him (Christ) were *all things* created." In view of the fact that the creative work is here ascribed to Christ, some venture the opinion that the expression "all things" (*panta*) refers to all the *new creation,* though the context rather favors the idea that the universe is meant. Now, the question arises, whether there is any passage in which the work of creation is ascribed to Christ, and the possibility of a reference to the new creation is excluded. Such a passage is found in I Cor. 8:6, where the phrase *ta panta* is used of all created things, and the creative work is ascribed equally to the Father and the Son. In Isa. 9:6 the prophet says: "For unto us a child is born . . . and his name shall be called . . . Mighty God (El gibbor)." Gesenius finds no reference to God here, and renders these words "mighty hero." But in Isa. 10:21, the same phrase is employed in a context, in which it can only refer to Deity. John 9:39 contains the statement: "For judgment I am come into the world, that they which see not might see, and that they which see might be made blind." Now, the word *krima* (judgment) quite generally denotes a judgment of condemnation. But the final clause in this case would seem to demand the broader signification of judgment in general, and the question arises, whether the word is ever used in that sense. Rom. 11:33 gives the answer to that question, for there the same word undoubtedly has a general signification.

b. *Parallels of words or phrases improperly so called.* These may be called improper parallels insofar as they do not contain the same, but synonymous words or expressions. Those cases in which an expression is more complete in one passage than in another, may also be put in this class. In II Sam.

8:18 we read: ". . . and David's sons were *cohanim"* (generally rendered, *priests*). Gesenius asserts that the word always means *priests,* while Fuerst contends that it may mean *principes, praefecti, sensu civili.* The latter's opinion is borne out by the parallel passage in I Chron. 18:17, where, in an enumeration similar to that of II Sam. 8, we read: "—and the sons of David were princes (*ri'shonim*)." Matt. 8:24 reads: "And behold, there arose a great *seismos."* This word really means earthquake, but the connection here seems to point to a different meaning. And this is confirmed by the parallel passages, Mark 4:37 and Luke 8:25, where the word *lailaps* is used, meaning a whirlwind, or a tempestuous wind. Again, in Heb. 1:3 we read: ". . . when He had by himself (*di' heautou*) purged our sins." The pregnant expression *di' heautou* is explained by the parallel passage in Heb. 9:26, which says: ". . . to put away sin by the sacrifice of himself."

EXERCISE: Determine the meaning of the following words in the connection in which they are found by means of the internal helps that were described "house" (*oikia*), II Cor. 5:1 "faith" (*pistis*), Heb. 11:1; "the veil" (*katapetasma*), Heb. 10:20; "shall overshadow thee," Luke 1:35; "the foundations of the world," Ps. 19:15; "a Jew," Rom. 2:28, 29; "were made" (*egeneto*), John 1:3, comp. Col. 1:16; "bring . . . into a snare," Prov. 29:8; "the elements of the world" (*stoicheia tou kosmou*), Gal. 4:3, comp. verse 9; "the hidden things of darkness" (*ta krupta tou skopou*), I Cor. 4:5; "flesh and blood" (*sarks kai haima*), I Cor. 15:50; comp. Matt. 16:17 and Gal. 1:16.

LITERATURE: TERRY, *Bib. Herm.,* pp. 79-88; 119-128; Immer. *Hermeneutics,* pp. 159-183; Muenscher, *Manual,* pp. 107-128; Davidson, *Sacred Herm.,* pp. 225-252; Elliott, *Bib. Herm.* pp. 101-116; Fairbairn, *Herm.,* pp. 79-106; Lutz, *Bib. Herm.,* pp. 186-226.

D. The Figurative Use of Words

1. PRINCIPAL TROPES USED IN SCRIPTURE. In the present connection we are not concerned with figures of syntax or

figures of thought, but rather with those figures of speech that are commonly called *tropes,* in which a word or expression is used in a different sense from that which properly belongs to it. They are founded on resemblance or on certain definite relations. The principal tropes are the metaphor, the metonymy, and the synecdoche.

a. *The metaphor* might be called an unexpressed comparison. It is a figure of speech in which one object is likened to another by asserting it to be that other, or by speaking of it as if it were that other. It differs from the simile in that it does not express the word of likeness. Metaphors are of frequent occurrence in the Bible. In Ps. 18:2, six of them are found in a single verse. Jesus employs this figure of speech when He says to the Pharisees: "Go ye, and tell that *fox,*" Luke 13:32. There are two kinds of metaphors in the Bible that have reference to the Divine Being and deserve special attention: (1) anthropopathisms and (2) anthropomorphisms. In the former, human emotions, passions and desires are ascribed to God. Cf. Gen. 6:6; Deut. 13:17; Eph. 4:30. In the latter, bodily members and physical activities are attributed to Him. Cf. Ex. 15:16; Ps. 34:16; Lam. 3:56; Zech. 14:4; Jas. 5:4. Undoubtedly there is also a great deal that is metaphorical in the description of heaven as a city with golden streets and pearly gates, in which the tree of life yields its fruits from month to month; and in the representation of the eternal torments as a worm that dieth not, a fire that is not quenched, and a smoke of torment ascending forever and ever.

b. *The metonymies* are also numerous in the Bible. This figure, as well as the synecdoche, is founded on a relation rather than on a resemblance. In the case of the metonymy, this relation is a mental rather than a physical one. It indicates such relations as cause and effect, progenitor and posterity, subject and attribute, sign and thing signified. Paul says in

I Thess. 5:19, "Quench not the *Spirit*," when he refers to the special manifestations of the Spirit. And when, in the parable of Dives and Lazarus, Abraham says, "They have *Moses* and the *Prophets*," Luke 16:29, he naturally means their writings. In Isa. 22:22, "the *key* of the house of David," conveys the idea of control over the royal house. Circumcision is called a *covenant* in Acts 7:8, because it was a sign of the covenant.

c. *The synecdoche* resembles the metonymy somewhat, but the relation on which it is founded is physical rather than mental. In this figure there is a certain identity of what is expressed and what is meant. A part is put for a whole, or a whole for a part; a genus for a species, or a species for a genus; an individual for a class, or a class for an individual; a plural for a singular, or a singular for a plural. Jephthah is said to have been buried "in the *cities* of Gilead" (Judg. 12: 7), when, of course, only one city was meant. When the prophet says in Dan. 12:2: "And many of those that sleep in the dust of the earth shall awake," he certainly did not intend to teach a partial resurrection. And when Luke informs us in Acts 27:37 that there were in all in the ship "two hundred, threescore and sixteen *souls*," he does not mean to intimate that there were only disembodied spirits aboard.

2. INTERNAL HELPS FOR DETERMINING WHETHER THE FIGURATIVE OR LITERAL SENSE IS INTENDED. It is of the greatest importance for the interpreter to know whether a word is used in a literal or in a figurative sense. The Jews, and even the disciples, often made serious mistakes by interpreting literally what Jesus meant figuratively. Cf. John 4:11,32; 6: 52; Matt: 16:6-12. Failure to understand that the Lord spoke figuratively when he said, "This (is) my body," even became a fruitful source of division in the Churches of the Reformation. Therefore, it is of paramount importance that the interpreter

have certainty on this point. The following considerations may aid him materially in settling this question.

a. There are certain writings in which the use of figurative language is *a priori* impossible. Among those are laws and all kinds of legal instruments, historical writings, philosophical and strictly scientific works, and Confessions. These aim primarily at clearness and precision, and make beauty a secondary consideration. Yet it is well to bear in mind that the prose of Orientals is far more figurative than that of Western people.

b. There is an old and oft-repeated Hermeneutical rule, that the words should be understood in their literal sense, unless such literal interpretation involves a manifest contradiction or absurdity. It should be observed, however, that in practice this becomes merely an appeal to every man's rational judgment. What seems absurd or improbable to one, may be regarded as perfectly simple and self-consistent by another.

c. The most important means to determine whether a word is used literally or figuratively in a certain connection is found in the internal helps to which we have already referred. The interpreter should have strict regard to the immediate context, to the adjuncts of a word, to the character of the subject and the predicates ascribed to it, to the parallelism, if it is present, and to the parallel passages.

3. PRINCIPLES USEFUL IN INTERPRETING FIGURATIVE LANGUAGE OF THE BIBLE. Now the question arises as to the interpretation of the figurative language of the Bible. While the interpreter must employ the regular internal helps that were just mentioned, there are certain special points which he should not fail to observe.

a. *It is of the greatest importance that the interpreter have a clear conception of the things on which the figures are based, or from which they are borrowed, since the tropical use of words is founded on certain resemblances or relations.* The figurative language of the Bible is derived especially from (1) the physical features of the Holy Land, (2) the religious institutions of Israel, (3) the history of God's ancient people, and (4) the daily life and customs of the various peoples that occupy a prominent place in the Bible. Therefore, these must be understood, in order to interpret the figures that are derived from them. In Ps. 92:12 we read: "The righteous shall flourish like the palm tree; he shall grow like a cedar in Lebanon." The expositor cannot hope to interpret this passage unless he is acquainted with the characteristics of the palm tree and the cedar. If he desires to explain Ps. 51:9: "Purge me with hyssop, and I shall be clean," he must have some knowledge of the method of ceremonial purification among Israel.

b. *The interpreter should make it a point to discover the principal idea, the tertium comparationis, without placing too much importance on the details.* When the Biblical authors employed such figures as metaphors, they generally had some specific point or points of agreement in mind. And even if the interpreter can find still more points of agreement, he must limit himself to those intended by the author. In Rom. 8:17, Paul says, in a transport of assurance: "And if children, then heirs; heirs of God and joint heirs with Christ." It is perfectly evident that he refers to the blessings which believers receive with Christ from their common Father. The metaphor contained in the word "heir" would be pressed too far, if it were made to imply the death of the Father as the testator. How dangerous it would be to apply a figure in all particulars appears very clearly from a passage like Rev. 16:15, where we read: "Behold, I come as a thief." The connection will generally determine in each particular case how far a figure should be applied.

c. *In connection with the figurative language that refers to God and the eternal order of things, the interpreter should bear in mind that it generally offers but a very inadequate expression of the perfect reality.* God is called a Light, a Rock, a Fortress, a high Tower, a Sun and a Shield. All these figures convey some idea of what God is for his people; but not a single one of them, nor taken together, give a complete representation of God. And when the Bible pictures the redeemed as clad in the garments of salvation, robed in the robe of righteousness, crowned with the crown of life, and bearing the palms of victory, the figures do indeed give us some, but only a very imperfect idea of their future glory.

d. *To a certain extent, one can test one's insight into the figures of the Bible by attempting to express the thoughts which they convey in literal language.* But it is necessary to bear in mind that a great deal of the figurative language of the Bible defies all such efforts. This applies particularly to the language in which the Bible speaks of God and eternal things. Diligent and careful study of the Bible will help us more than anything else to understand the figurative language of the Bible.

EXERCISE: What kind of figures have the writers used in the following passages, and how must they be interpreted: Gen. 49:14; Num. 24:21; Deut. 32:40; Job 34:6, "my arrow is incurable"; Ps. 26:6; Ps. 46:9; Ps. 108:9; Eccles. 12:3, "day"; Jer. 2:13; Jer. 8:7; Ezek. 7:27; Ezek. 23:29; Zech. 7:11; Matt. 3:5; Matt. 5:13; Matt. 12:40; Rom. 6:4; I Cor. 5:7, 8.

LITERATURE: Terry, *Bib. Herm.,* pp. 157-176; Davidson, *Sacred Herm.,* pp. 284-319; Muenscher, *Manual,* pp. 145-166; Elliott, *Bib. Herm.,* pp. 142-151; Fairbairn, *Herm. Manual,* pp. 157-173.

E. The Interpretation of the Thought

From the interpretation of the separate words we proceed to that of the words in their mutual relation, or of the thought. For the present however, we are concerned only with the formal expression of the thought, and not with its material contents.   The discussion of the latter is postponed until the Historical and Theological interpretation call for consideration. The explanation of the thought is sometimes called "logical interpretation."   It proceeds on the assumption that the language of the Bible is, like every other language, a product of the human spirit, developed under providential guidance. This being so, it is perfectly evident that the Bible must be interpreted according to the same logical principles that are applied in the interpretation of other writings.

The points which call for consideration here are (1) the special idioms and the figures of thought, (2) the order of words in a sentence, (3) the special significance of various cases and prepositions, (4) the logical connection of the different clauses and sentences, and (5) the course of thought in an entire section.

1. THE SPECIAL IDIOMS AND FIGURES OF THOUGHT. Every language has certain characteristic expression, called idioms. The Hebrew language forms no exception to the rule, and some of its idioms are carried over into the New Testament. There is a frequent use of the hendiadys. Thus we read in I Sam. 2:3: "Thou shalt not multiply, thou shalt not speak." This evidently means, thou shalt not multiply words.   In his defense before the Sanhedrin, Paul says: " . . . of the hope and resurrection of the dead I am called in question" (Acts 23:6). The meaning is, "of the hope of the resurrection . . ." Then, too, a noun in the genitive often takes the place of an adjective.   Moses urges the objection to his commission that he is not "a man of words," i.e., an eloquent man (Ex. 4:10). And Paul, in writing to the Thessalonians, speaks of their "patience of hope," when he means their patient hope, hope characterized by patience.   Furthermore, when in the Old Testament the words *lo' kol* are written together, they must be rendered, *not all;* but when they are separated by intervening

words, they should be translated, *none, nothing.* It would be a serious mistake to render Ps. 143:2, "Not every living one shall be justified in thy sight," though this would be a literal translation. The evident meaning is, "No man living shall be justified in thy sight." Cf. also Ps. 103:2. Similar cases are found in the New Testament. Cf. Matt. 24:22; Mark 13:20; Luke 1:37; John 3:15,16; 6:39; 12:46; Rom. 3:20; I Cor. 1:29; Gal. 2:16; I John 2:21; Rev. 18:22.

There are also several kinds of figures of thought that deserve special attention.

a. *Some figures promote a lively representation of the truth.*

(1) *The simile.* How vivid the picture of complete destruction in Ps. 2:9: " . . . thou shalt dash them to pieces like a potter's vessel"; and that of utter loneliness in Isa. 1:8: "And the daughter of Zion is left as a cottage in a vineyard." Cf. also Ps. 102:6; Cant. 2:9.

(2) *The allegory,* which is merely an extended metaphor, and should be interpreted on the same general principles. Examples of it are found in Ps. 80:8-15; and John 10:1-18. Terry makes the following distinction between the allegory and the parable: "The allegory is a figurative use and application of some supposable fact or history, whereas, the parable is itself such a supposable fact or history. The parable uses words in their literal sense, and its narrative never transgresses the limits of what might have been actual fact. The allegory is continually using words in a metaphorical sense, and its narrative, however supposable in itself, is manifestly fictitious."

b. *Other figures promote brevity of expression.* They result from the rapidity and energy of the author's thought, which fosters a desire to omit all superfluous words.

(1) *The ellipsis,* which consists in the omission of a word or words, necessary to the complete construction of a sentence,

but not required for the understanding of it. Moses prays, "Return, O Jehovah—How long?" (wilt thou desert us?) The short, abrupt sentences reveal the poet's emotion. For other examples, cf. I Cor. 6:13; II Cor. 5:13; Ex. 32:32; Gen. 3:22.

(2) *Brachylogy*, also a concise or abridged form of speech, consisting especially in the non-repetition or omission of a word, when its repetition or use would be necessary to complete the grammatical construction. In this figure, the omission is not as noticeable as in the ellipsis. Thus Paul says in Rom. 11:18: "Boast not against the branches. But if thou boast, thou bearest not the root, but the root (bears) thee." Notice also I John 5:9: "If we receive the witness of men, the witness of God is greater."

(3) *The Constructio Praegnans,* in which a preposition is joined with an expressed verb, while it really belongs to an unexpressed verb which is included in the other as its consequent. For instance, in Ps. 74:7, we read: "They have cast fire into thy sanctuary, they have *defiled* the dwellingplace of thy name *to the ground."* The thought must be completed in some such way as, *razing or burning it to the* ground. Paul says in II Tim. 4:18: "he (the Lord) will *save me* (bringing me) *into his kingdom."*

(4) *The Zeugma*, consisting of two nouns that are construed with one verb, though only one of them—usually the first—directly suits the verb. Thus we read literally in I Cor. 3:2: "Milk I caused thee to drink, and not meat." And in Luke 1:64 we are told respecting Zacharias: "And his mouth was opened immediately, and his tongue." In supplying the missing words, the interpreter must exercise great care, lest he change the sense of that which is written.

c. *Still other figures aim at softening an expression.* They find their explanation in the author's delicacy of feeling or modesty.

(1) *Euphemism* consists in substituting a less offensive word for one that expresses more accurately what is meant. "And when he said this, he fell asleep" (Acts 7:60).

(2) *The Litotes* affirms a thing by the negation of the opposite. Thus the psalmist sings: "A broken and a contrite heart, O God, thou wilt not despise" (Ps. 51:17). And Isaiah says: "A bruised reed shall He not break, and the smoking flax shall He not quench" (Isa. 42:3).

(3) *The Meiosis* is closely related to the litotes. Some authorities identify the two; others regard the litotes as a species of meiosis. It is a figure of speech in which less is said than is meant. Cf. I Thess. 2:15; II Thess. 32; Heb. 13:17.

d. *Finally, there are figures that give more point to an expression, or that strengthen it.* They may be the result of righteous indignation or of a lively imagination.

(1) *Irony* contains censure or ridicule under cover of praise or compliment. Cf. Job. 12:2; I Kings 22:15; I Cor. 4:6. There are cases in the Bible in which irony has passed into sarcasm. Cf. I Sam. 26:15; I Kings 18:27; I Cor. 4:8.

(2) *Epizeuxis* strengthens an expression by the simple repetition of a word (Gen. 22:11; II Sam. 16:7; Isa. 40:1).

(3) *Hyperbole* is of frequent occurrence, and consists of a rhetorical over-statement (Gen. 22:17; Deut. 1:28; II Chron. 28:4).

2. THE ORDER OF WORDS IN A SENTENCE. "The arrangement of the several words in a sentence," says Winer, "is in general determined by the order in which the conceptions are formed, and by the closer relation in which certain parts of the sentence stand to one another." It frequently happens, how-

ever, that the Biblical writers, for some reason or other, depart from the usual arrangement. In some cases they do this for rhetorical effect; in others, to bring certain concepts into closer relation with each other. But there are also cases in which the desire to emphasize a certain word led to its transposition. These instances are particularly important for the interpreter. The context will usually reveal the reason for the change that was brought about.

In the Hebrew verbal sentence, the regular order is: Predicate, subject, object. If in such a sentence the object stands first, or the subject is placed at the beginning or at the end, it is highly probable that they are emphatic. The first place is the most important one in the sentence, but the emphatic word may also occupy the last place. Harper gives the following variations from the usual order:

(a) object, predicate, subject, which emphasizes the object (I Kings 14:11);

(b) object, subject, predicate, which likewise emphasizes the object (Gen. 37:16);

(c) subject, object, predicate, which emphasizes the subject (Gen. 17:9); and

(d) predicate, object, subject, which also emphasizes the subject (I Sam. 15:33).

In the nominal sentences, which describe a condition rather than an action, the usual order is: subject, predicate, whenever the predicate is a noun. The regular order is found, for example, in Deut. 4:35, "Jehovah (He) is God." But in Gen. 12:13 the author departs from the usual arrangement: "Say, I pray thee, my sister thou art." Here the predicate is made emphatic.

But the Hebrew language has still more effective means of expressing emphasis. The function of the infinitive absolute in this respect is so well known as to need no illustration. The greatest prominence is given to a substantive by permitting it to stand, absolutely, at the beginning of the sentence, and then representing it, in its proper place, by a pronoun. Cf. Gen. 47:21: ". . . the people, he removed them" and Ps. 18:3: "God, . . . perfect is his way." Sometimes an idea is first expressed by a pronoun, and then resumed by a noun, as in Jos. 1:2, ". . the land which I give to them, the children of Israel."

Similar principles apply in the interpretation of the New Testament. In the Greek language, the subject with its modifiers ordinarily occupies the first place: it is followed by the predicate with its adjuncts. The object generally follows the verb: an adjective, the substantive to which it belongs; and a genitive, its governing noun. If the order is changed, it means, in all probability, that some word is made emphatic. This is clearly the case, where the predicate stands first, as in Rom. 8:18, ". . . that not worthy are the sufferings of the present time." Cf. also Matt. 5:3-11; II Tim. 2:11. For the same purpose, the object is sometimes placed in the foreground, as in Luke 16:11, ". . . the true (riches) who commit to your trust?" Cf. also John 9:31; Rom. 14:1. Again, the same end is served by placing a genitive before its governing noun, or an attributive adjective before the substantive to which it belongs. Thus we read in Rom. 11:13: "I am of gentiles an apostle." Cf. also Rom. 12:19; Heb. 6:16. And in Matt. 7:13, the admonition reads: "Enter ye in at the strait (adj. first) gate."

3. THE SPECIAL SIGNIFICATION OF THE CASES AND THE PREPOSITIONS. The expositor must take particular notice of certain combinations of words, such as prepositional phrases, and phrases in which a genitive or dative occurs. Questions such as the following must be answered: Is the genitive in Ezekiel 12:19, ". . . the violence of all who are dwelling in it," a subjective or an objective genitive? How about that in Oba-

diah, verse 10, ". . . the violence of thy brother Jacob"; and that in Gen. 18:20, ". . . . the cry of Sodom and Gomorrah"? What kind of a genitive have we in Isa. 37:22, ". . . the virgin of the daughter of Zion"? Are the following genitives subjective or objective: John 5:42, "the love of God"; Phil. 4:7, "the peace of God"; and Rom. 4:13, "the righteousness of faith"? How should those in Rom. 8:23, "the firstfruits of the Spirit," and in Rev. 2:10 "a crown of life," be interpreted? The dative may also give rise to several questions. A few examples must suffice. Is the dative in Rom. 8:24, "for in (or, by) hope we are saved," modal or instrumental? Must the dative found in Phil. 1:27, ". . . striving together for (or, by) the faith of the gospel," be regarded as a *dative commodi* or *instrumentalis*?

Prepositional phrases may also raise important questions. The special meaning of some prepositions depends on the case with which they are used. Moreover, there are some prepositions that have a similar meaning, and yet reveal characteristic differences. The interpreter cannot afford to neglect these fine distinctions. Since the preposition occupies a far more important place in the Greek than in the Hebrew language, we limit ourselves to New Testament examples. In I Cor. 15:15 we read: "And we are also found false witnesses, because we did testify of (Gr., *kata*) God, that He raised up Christ . . ." Is the rendering "of" correct, or should it be "against" (Meyer), or "by" as in Matt. 26:63? What is the meaning of the same preposition in Rom. 8:27, *"kata theon"*; and in Heb. 11:13, "These all died in (kata) faith"? Should the last passage read, "in" or "according to," or "conformably to faith"? (As many commentators say). What does the preposition *apo* mean in Heb. 5:7, "and was heard *apo* fear"? Should it be rendered "out of" i.e., "heard, delivering him out of fear" (constructio praegnans); or is it better to translate, " . . . in respect to what he feared"; or still different, ". . . on account of godly fear"? How should *en* be interpreted in the phrase, "in Christ," (Rom. 8:2 Gal. 1:22 2:17); and *eis* in the expression, "in the name," (Matt. 28:19)? Are *eis* and *en* used interchangeably, or do they always differ in signification? What is the meaning of *eis* after verbs of rest, and that of *en* after verbs of motion? How does *dia tes charitos* (Rom. 12:3), differ from *dia ten charin* (Rom. 15:15)? What is the meaning of *dia* in John 6:57, "even he shall live *di' eme*"? In Rom. 3:30 the apostle says that God "shall justify the circumcision by (*ek*) faith, and the uncircumcision through (*dia*) faith." What is the difference in meaning? How do the prepositions *anti*, *huper* and *peri* differ, when they are used in relation to the work of Christ in connection with sin or in the interest of sinners? Comp. Matt. 20:28; I Cor. 15:3; Rom. 5:6; Gal. 1:4. Again, how should *huper* and *peri* be distinguished, when they are used in connection with prayer for others? Cf. Matt. 5:44; I Thess. 5:25.

4. THE LOGICAL CONNECTION OF THE DIFFERENT CLAUSES AND SENTENCES. It is absolutely necessary that the interpreter have a clear conception of the logical relation in which the various clauses and sentences stand to each other. To that end he will have to study the use of the participles and the conjunctions.

a. *The relation indicated by the participle.* This may be:

(1) *Modal*: Matt. 19:22, ". . . he went away, being sorrowful"; Acts 2:13, ". . . others, mocking said."

(2) *Causal*: Acts 4:21, ". . . they let them go, finding nothing" (i.e., because they found nothing).

(3) *Conditional*: Rom. 2:27, "And shall not uncircumcision, . . . fulfilling the law (i.e., if it fulfill the law), judge thee?"

(4) *Concessive*: Rom. 1:32, "Who, knowing the judgment of God (i.e., though they know), not only do the same."

(5) *Temporal*: expressing either antecedent, simultaneous, or consequent action. Important exegetical questions may rise in this connection. In John 3:13 the Lord says to Nicodemus: "And no man hath ascended up to heaven, but he that came down from heaven, even the Son of Man which is (present participle) in heaven. Is it correct to render the participle by "is," or should it be "was"? Again, in II Cor. 8:9, the apostle says: "For ye know the grace of our Lord Jesus Christ, that, being rich (present participle), yet for your sake He became poor." Is this rendering correct, or should it be, "Though He was rich . . ." The answer to such questions will depend on the context. The participle itself is timeless. The only question arising is that of its time relative to that of the finite verb. The following rules, derived from Burton's *New Testament Moods and Tenses*, p. 174, are valuable:

(a) "If the action of the participle is antecedent to that of the verb, the participle most commonly precedes the verb, but not invariably. Such a participle is usually in the Aorist tense, but occasionally in the present."

(b) "If the action of the participle is simultaneous with that of the verb, it may either precede or follow the verb, more frequently the latter. It is of course in the present tense." (This statement of Burton's needs correction. There are many cases in the New Testament in which the aorist participle and the main verb denote *coincident* or *identical* action. Cf. Matt. 22:1; Acts 10:33. Cf. Moulton, *Prolegomena*, p. 133; Robertson, *Grammar of the Greek New Testament*, p. 1112 f.)

(c) "If the action of the participle is subsequent to that of the principal verb, it almost invariably follows the verb, the tense of the participle being determined by the conception of the action as respects its progress." (There is no proof for an aorist of subsequent action. Cf. Moulton, *Proleg.*, p. 132; Robertson, *Grammar*, p. 1113.)

b. *The relation indicated by the conjunctions.* The most important means of connecting clauses and sentences are the conjunctions. They furnish the clearest and most decisive index to the logical relation in which the thoughts stand to each other. Their value, as an aid to interpretation, increases with their specificness. The more numerous their meanings, the more difficult it becomes to determine the precise relation which they indicate. The Hebrew *vav,* which serves as a *conjunctio generalis,* offers very little aid. Another difficulty arises from the fact that, in certain instances, one conjunction is apparently used for another.

The conjunction *hoti* serves to introduce either a causal or an objective clause, so that the question arises as to whether it should be rendered "because" or "that." As a rule, the context will readily answer that question. It makes very little difference how it is conceived of in John 7:23, but in Rom. 8:21 the case is different. The apostle says: "For the creature was made subject to vanity, not willingly, but by reason of him who hath subjected the same in hope, that (or, because) the creature itself shall also be delivered." It all depends on the conception of *hoti,* whether the last words describe the contents of the hope, or give a reason for it. Some grammarians claim that *hina* is always final in the New Testament, and therefore introduces a clause of purpose. But though this is undoubtedly its usual meaning, it cannot be maintained throughout. These are cases in which it is practically equivalent to *hoti.* Cf. Matt. 10:25; Luke 1:43; John 4:34. Moreover, it is also used in an ecbatic sense, to express a contemplated result. This is the case in Gal. 5:17, ". . . so that ye cannot do the things that ye would"; and in I Thess. 5:4, "But ye, brethren, are not in darkness, that (*hina*) that day should overtake you as a thief."

Though it is true that the Biblical authors occasionally depart from the ordinary use of a conjunction—and the interpreter should be ready to admit this—he should never be hasty in ascribing a meaning to a conjunction that is not warranted linguistically. It is an arbitrary procedure to render *ki* in Isa. 5:10 "yea," seeing that the conjunction is not known to have an explicative meaning, and the usual sense is perfectly appropriate. In the interpretation of Luke 7:47, "Wherefore I say unto thee, Her sins are forgiven, which are many; for (*hoti*) she loved much," some expositors were prompted by their dogmatical views to ascribe to the conjunction the meaning of *dio,* (wherefore), though it never occurs in that sense.

It should be borne in mind that the assumption of some of the older exegetes, to the effect that the writers of the New Testament often confounded the conjunctions, and, for example, used *de* for *gar,* and vice versa, is altogether unwarranted. Careful study will usually reveal a discriminating choice. Cf. the various grammars of the New Testament.

Moreover, it is necessary to guard against the mistake that a conjunction always connects a thought with the one immediately preceding it. In Matt. 10:31 we read: "Fear ye not therefore, ye are of more value than many sparrows." And immediately following this: "Whosoever therefore shall confess me before men . . ." This is an inference, not from the exhortation in the 31st verse, but from all that was said from the 16th verse on. Similarly, in Eph. 2:11-13, the "wherefore" with which the passage begins does not connect the 11th with the 10th verse, but with the propositions in the verses 1-7.

Finally, there are passages that are not connected by conjunctions. In some cases, they are not logically related to one another, as in Luke 16:15-18. Compare v. 16 with Matt. 11:12, 13; v. 17 with Matt. 5:18; and v. 18 with Matt. 5:32. In other instances, however, they are clearly related, as in Matt. 5:2-11; and I John 1:8-10. In such cases it is necessary to discover the connection by a diligent study of the course of thought, and of the arrangement of the words in the sentence.

5. THE COURSE OF THOUGHT OF AN ENTIRE SECTION. It is not sufficient that the interpreter fixes his attention on the separate clauses and sentences; he must acquaint himself with the general thought of the writer or speaker. Sometimes it taxes his ability to follow the reasoning of the Biblical authors. We do not refer to the peculiar difficulties encountered in the interpretation of the Prophets. Other parts of Scripture also present *cruces interpretum*. The separate thoughts may appear unrelated, while, in fact, they are closely connected. There are cases in which it seems to some that the course of thought is not in harmony with the laws of logic. Sometimes the discourse as a whole apparently suffers from inherent contradiction. A single example may serve to illustrate the difficulty which we have in mind. In John 3, Nicodemus is seen to approach Jesus with the words: "Rabbi, we know that thou art a teacher come from God; for no man can do those signs which thou doest, except God be with him." How is Jesus' answer in the 3rd verse related to these words? In the 4th verse Nicodemus declares that he does not understand Jesus. Does the Lord answer his question in the verses 5-8? The Pharisee repeats his question in the 9th verse, and Jesus expresses surprise at his ignorance in verse 10. Why does He now point to the fact that He knows whereof He speaks: to the unbelief of the Jews, including Nicodemus; and to his coming from heaven and his future exaltation on the cross

for the salvation of believers? Do the verses 16-21 also contain the words of Jesus? Cf. also John 8:31-37; Gal. 2:11-21.

The parables deserve special attention. The word "parable" is derived from the Greek *paraballo* (*to throw or place by the side of*), and suggests the idea of placing one thing by the side of the other for comparison. It denotes a symbolic method of speech, in which a moral or spiritual truth is illustrated by the analogy of common experience. But while the parable is essentially a comparison, a simile, all similies are not parables. The parable limits itself to that which is real, and in its imagery does not go beyond the limits of probability, or of what might be actual fact. It keeps the two elements of comparison distinct as "an inner and outer," and does not attribute the qualities and relations of the one to the other. In this respect it differs from the allegory, which is really an extended metaphor and contains its interpretation within itself. The Lord had a twofold purpose in using the parables, viz., to reveal the mysteries of the Kingdom of God to his disciples, and to conceal them from those who had no eye for the realities of the spiritual world.

In the interpretation of the parable, three elements must be taken in consideration.

a. *The scope of the parable, or the thing to be illustrated.* It is of primary importance that the purpose of the parable stand out clearly in the mind of the interpreter. In his attempt to discover it, he should not overlook the important helps that are offered in the Bible.

(1) The occasion on which a parable is introduced may illustrate its meaning and bearing. Matt. 20:1 ff. is explained by 19:27; Matt. 25:14 ff., by verse 13; Luke 16:19-31 by the 14th verse. Cf. also Luke 10:29; 15:1, 2; and 19:11, for the purpose of the following parables.

(2) The object of the parable may be expressly stated in the introduction, as in Luke 18:1.

(3) Certain expressions at the end of a parable may also indicate its bearing. Cf. Matt. 13:49; Luke 11:9; 12:21.

(4) Again a similar parable of similar import may point out the thing to be illustrated. Compare Luke 15:3 ff. with Matt. 18:12 ff. The 14th verse of Matt. 18 contains a valuable hint.

(5) In many cases, however, the interpreter will have to discover the purpose of a parable by the careful study of its context.

b. *The figurative representation of the parable.* After the scope of the parable is determined, the figurative representation calls for close scrutiny. The formal narrative that is meant at once to reveal and to conceal the truth must be analyzed carefully, and all the necessary geographical, archaeological, and historical light, must be brought to bear upon it.

c. *The tertium comparationis.* Finally, the *tertium comparationis,* the exact point of comparison must be detected. There is always some special aspect of the Kingdom of God, some particular line of duty to be followed, or some danger to be shunned, which the parable seeks to exhibit, and to which all its imagery is subservient. As long as the interpreter has not discovered this point, he cannot hope to understand the parable, and he should not try to explain the individual traits, for these can be seen in their true light only when contemplated in relation to the central idea. Moreover, great care should be taken not to ascribe independent spiritual significance to all the details of the parable. It is impossible to state precisely how far an expositor may go in this respect. The question of just what in the parable belongs to the ethical or doctrinal contents, and what to the mere delineation, does not admit of a clear-cut answer. A great deal must be left to common sense. The interpreter must make it a point to discriminate carefully. Failure to do this often led and is bound to lead to fanciful and arbitrary interpretations. In a general way, the rule laid down by Immer may be of some service: "What ministers to the fundamental thought or the intention of the parable, belongs to the doctrinal contents, but what does not minister thereto, is mere delineation." It will be instructive in this matter to study the explanations which the Lord gave of the parable of the Sower, and of that of the Wheat and the Tares.

EXERCISE: What idiomatic expressions are found in the following passages: Gen. 1:14; 19:9; 31:15; Jer. 7:13; Gal. 2:16; John 3:29; Rev. 2:17; 18:22?

Name and interpret the figures of thought that are found in the following passages: Job 12:2; Ps. 32:9; 102:7; Prov. 14:34; Isa. 42:3; 55:12; Matt. 7:24-27; Acts 4:28; John 21:25; Rom. 9:29; I Cor. 4:8; 11:22; II Cor. 6:8-10.

What significant change in the order of words is found in the following passages? Ps. 3:5 (Heb.); 18:31 (Heb.); 74:17; Jer. 10:6; Matt. 13:28; John 17:4; I Cor. 2:7; II Tim. 2:11; Heb. 6:16; 7:4?

Notice the following examples of anacolutha: Gen. 3:22; Ps. 18:48, 49; Zech. 2:11; Rom. 8:3 (Winer-Moulton, p. 718); Gal. 2:6; II Pet. 2:4-9.

Explain the genitives and datives in the following passages: Gen. 47: 43; 1 Kings 10:9; Prov. 20:2; Rom. 1:17; 10:4; Col. 2:18; Rom. 8:24.

What is the meaning of the following prepositions? *dia,* in Rom. 3:25; I Cor. 1:9; Heb. 3:16; Rev. 4:11; *en,* in Matt. 11:11; Acts 7:29; Rev. 5:9; *anti,* in Matt. 2:22; 20:28; *huper,* in Gal. 1:4; II Cor. 5:21; Heb. 5:1; *peri,* in I Cor. 16:12, III John 2; *eis,* in Mark 1:39; Acts 19:22; 20:29; John 8:30.

How is the participle related to the finite verb in I Cor. 9:19; 11:29; Matt. 1:19; 27:49; Luke 22:65; Acts 1:24.

What is the force of the following conjunctions? *kai,* in Matt. 5:25; John 1:16; I Cor. 3:5; *alla,* in I Cor. 15:35; II Cor. 11:1;

hoti, in Matt. 5:45; John 2:18; *gar.* in Matt. 2:2; John 9:30; *de* in I Cor. 15:13; 4:7; *hina,* in John 4:36; 5:20; Rom. 11:31; I Thess. 5:4.

LITERATURE: Terry, *Bib. Herm.,* pp. 166-243; Immer, *Hermeneutics,* pp. 198-235; Davidson, *Sacred Herm.,* pp. 252-319; Fairbairn, *Herm. Manual,* pp. 173-189; the New Testament Grammars of Winer, Buttmann, Blass, Moulton, and Robertson.

F. Internal Helps for the Interpretation of the Thought

The Bible itself contains some helps for the logical interpretation of its contents, and the interpreter should not fail to make the most of these.

1. THE SPECIAL SCOPE OF THE AUTHOR. By this is meant the object he had in view in writing the particular portion of his work under consideration. The Biblical authors, of course, had a definite purpose in mind in the composition of the different parts of their writings, and aimed at the development of some special thought. And it is but natural to suppose that they chose such words and expressions as were best adapted to convey the intended meaning, and to contribute to the general argument. Therefore a thorough acquaintance with the special scope of the author will shed light even on minor details, on the use of participles and conjunctions, and of prepositional and adverbial phrases. It is hardly necessary to remark that, as the words and expressions must be studied in the light of the special scope of the author, so the special scope, in turn, must be seen against the background of the general scope, or the purpose which the author had in writing his book. This broader purpose will come up for consideration, when the historical interpretation of the Bible is considered.

Now the question arises as to the best method to discover the special scope. This is not always equally easy. Sometimes the author states it plainly. The particular purpose of the song of Moses, contained in Deut. 32, is clearly indicated in 31:19-21. Paul tells his readers in Rom. 11:14 why he is addressing the Gentiles in that particular section, and emphasizes their adoption by God. But in the majority of cases the special scope is not pointed out, and the interpreter will find it necessary to read and perhaps re-read a whole section, together with the preceding and following context in order to detect its purpose. Many a time the conclusion to which an author comes in the connection will reveal the purpose he has in mind. This is particularly true of the writings of Paul, in which logical reasoning predominates. Notice, *e.g.,* Rom. 2:1; 3:20, 28; 5:18; 8:1; 10:17; Gal. 3:9; 4:7,31. Moreover, it will be expedient to note carefully the occasion that leads to the argumentation in a certain section; for occasion and purpose are correlatives. The purpose Paul had in mind in writing the classical passage respecting the humiliation and exaltation of Christ, Phil. 2:6-11, is best understood in the light of what precedes in the verses 3 and 4. There the apostle admonishes the Philippians: "Let nothing be done through strife or vainglory; but in lowliness of mind let each esteem the other better than themselves. Look not every man on his own things, but every man also on the things of others." And then he continues: "Let this mind be in you, which was also in Christ Jesus . . . ," thus making it quite evident that he desires to present Christ to the Philippians as one who humbled himself, in order that He might serve others; who did not regard his own things exclusively, but also the things of others; and who ascended through the deepest humiliation to the highest glory.

2. THE CONNECTION. The absolute necessity of taking particular notice of the preceding and following, the near and remote connection of a passage, can scarcely be over-emphasized. It is the *conditio sine qua non* of all sound exegesis. And yet

this is often neglected, especially by those who regard the Bible as a collection of proof-texts. The division of the contents of Scripture into chapters and verses is always apt to endanger this conception. Consequently, many passages of the Bible were misinterpreted in the course of time, and these perversions were handed down from generation to generation. The following passages may serve as examples: Prov. 28:14; 31:6; Jer. 3:14b; Zech. 4:6b; Matt. 4:4b; 10:19; II Cor. 3:6b. Rev. E. Kropveld wrote an instructive little work on, "misbruikte Schriftuurplaatsen," which the interpreter can consult with profit. No interpretation that neglects the connection should be dignified with the name "exegesis."

The connection is not always of the same kind. Four types of connections merit attention:

(a) *Purely historical,* when one historical narrative follows another to which it is genetically and ideologically related (Matt. 3:13-17; 4:1-11).

(b) *Historico-dogmatical,* when a dogmatical discourse or teaching is connected with a historical fact (John 6:1-14, 26-65).

(c) *Logical,* in that the thoughts or arguments are presented in a strictly logical order (Rom. 5:1 ff.; I Cor. 15:12-19).

(d) *Psychological,* when the connection depends on the association of ideas. This often causes an apparent break in the line of thought (Heb. 5:11 ff).

a. In studying the connection, *close attention must be paid to the conjunctions.* By neglecting this, the interpreter may miss important points. We refrain from giving examples, but refer to what has already been said respecting the use of conjunctions. In some cases, the conjunction itself may represent an element of uncertainty, and the expositor will have to rely on the general context. For example, the conjunction *de* may be either continuative or adversative, and this makes it uncertain whether John 3:1 introduces Nicodemus as an illustration or as an exception.

b. *As a rule the connection should be sought as near as possible.* But if a passage does not yield good sense in connection with the immediately preceding, the more remote context must be consulted. Some commentators would connect Rom. 2:16 with the 15th verse. But this construction is very objectionable, and it is preferable to go back to the 12th or 13th verse, and to regard the intervening sentences as a parenthesis. On the other hand, some unnecessarily link Rom. 8:22 with the 19th verse, while it yields a perfectly good sense if connected with the 21st verse.

c. *When the connection is not at once apparent, the interpreter should not hastily conclude that there is a change in the course of thought, but rather pause and reflect.* On careful consideration it may become evident that there is only a seeming change, while in fact the same subject is continued. In I Cor. 8, Paul treats of the right use of Christian liberty in adiaphora. Now, it seems as if he turns away from this subject in 9:1, and begins with a defense of his apostleship, when he says: "Am I not an apostle?" etc. But this is only apparent. He points out that he, as an apostle of Jesus Christ, has many rights and liberties, but makes a considerate use of them, in order that his work may be more fruitful.

d. *The interpreter should have an open eye for parentheses, digressions and anacolutha.* These all disturb the connection more or less. In the case of *parentheses,* remarks relating to time and place, or brief secondary circumstances, are intercalated, after which a paragraph or sentence is continued, as if no interruption had taken place. Thus we read in Gen. 23:2: "And Sarah died in Kirjath-arba (the same is Hebron in the land of Canaan) and Abraham came to mourn for Sarah and to weep for her." Cf. also Isa. 52:14, 15; Dan. 8:2; Acts 1:15.

Digressions differ from parentheses in that they are longer and consist of deviations from the line of argument pursued into collateral topics, or in turning from the direct course of thought into another somewhat allied to it. There is a remarkable example in Eph. 3:2-13, which some would even extend to 4:1. Cf. also II Cor. 3:14-17; Heb. 5:10-7:1.

Anacolutha consist of an unexpected change from one construction to another, without completing the former. They are often expressive of energy or strong emotions. Cf. Zech. 2:11; Ps. 18:47, 48; Luke 5:14; I Tim. 1:3. Occasionally, an anacoluthon is connected with a parenthesis or digression, and then presents a double difficulty. In Rom. 5:12 the apostle says: "Wherefore, as by one man sin entered into the world, and death by sin; and so death passed upon all men, for that all have sinned." Now, he would naturally be expected to continue: "so also by one, Jesus Christ, righteousness entered, and through righteousness, life." But the apostle drops the thought in verse 12, and when he takes it up again in verse 18, the construction is changed.

e. *In cases in which the connection is not obvious, the question arises, whether the passage to be interpreted does not contain a reflection on, or an answer to the thoughts, as distinguished from the words, of the persons addressed; and whether there is not a possible psychological connection.* A careful study of the discourses and conversations of the Saviour reveals the fact that he often gave answer to the thoughts rather than to the words of his auditors. Cf. Luke 14:1-5: John 3:2; 5:17, 19, 41; 6:26. Many commentators have adjudged the words in Micah 2:12, 13 to be an interpolation, because of the seeming lack of connection. But it is quite possible to find a psychological connection here. The prophet warns the people of prophesying of wine and strong drink that seemed so desirable to many. And the thought of this apparent good gives him occasion to speak of the real blessings which the Lord would shower upon his people.

f. *The interpreter should gladly accept the explanations which the authors themselves occasionally give of their own words or of the words of the speakers, whom they introduce, in the immediate context.* It goes without saying that they are better qualified to speak with authority in this respect than anyone else. Examples of such interpretations are found in John 2:21: 7:29; 12:33; Rom. 7:18; Heb. 7:21.

3. PARALLELISM MAY ALSO AID IN THE INTERPRETATION OF THE THOUGHT. In employing it, the expositor must guard against two mistakes. On the one hand, against the assumption that each one of the parallel clauses has a meaning distinct from the other. This is the extreme to which some of the older interpreters went, since they regarded it as unbecoming to the wisdom of the Holy Spirit that the same thoughts or sentiments should be repeated. On the other hand, it is necessary to avoid the supposition that there is ever mere tautology, the parallel members containing exactly the same idea. It is a mistake to think that there is complete identity of meaning in the corresponding members of a synonymous parallelism, or an exact contrast in an antithetic parallelism. Regarding the former, Davidson correctly remarks: "Sometimes the one member expresses universally what the other announces particularly, or vice versa; in the one there may be the genus, in the other the species; the one expresses a thing affirmatively, the other negatively; the one figuratively, the other literally; the one has a comparison, the other its application; the one contains a fact, the other the manner in which it took place" (*Sacred Hermeneutics,* p. 234).

It is quite evident, therefore, that the exegetical function of parallelism consists "in its giving a general apprehension of the meaning of a clause rather than a precise or minute specification." In employing it the interpreter must be sure of the relative lucidity of the parallel members, lest he should make the mistake of trying to throw light on that which is less obscure by means of that which is dark and difficult to understand. If one member is figurative and the other literal, the latter should be used to elucidate the former.

A few examples may serve to illustrate its use. In Ps. 22:27 we read: "All the ends of the earth (world) shall remember and turn into the Lord, and all the kindreds of the nations shall worship before thee." The parallelism makes it perfectly evident that "the ends of the earth" refers to the distant nations, or Gentiles. Ps. 104:6 contains the enigmatic expression: "Thou coveredst it with the deep as with a garment"; but this is elucidated by the following words: "the waters stood above the mountains." In John 6:35, Jesus says: "I am the bread of Life; he that cometh to me shall never hunger." Here the question arises as to what kind of coming the Lord refers, and the following member of the parallelism answers this: "and he that believeth on me shall never thirst." II Cor. 5:21 contains an antithetic parallelism: "For He hath made him to be sin for us, who knew no sin; that we might be made the righteousness of God in him." Does the apostle mean that Christ was made sin for us in an ethical or in a legal sense? The antithesis, "that we might be made the righteousness of God in him," contains the answer, for this can be understood only in a legal sense.

G. External Helps for the Grammatical Interpretation

1. VALUABLE EXTERNAL HELPS. The external helps for the grammatical (including the logical) interpretation of Scripture, consist of the following:

a. *Grammars*

(1) For the Old Testament: Ewald, Gesenius-Kautzsch, Green, Wilson, Davidson, Harper, Noordtzij.

(2) For the New Testament: Winer (Eng. Winer-Moulton and Winer-Thayer), Buttmann (Eng. Buttmann-Thayer), Blass, Moulton, Robertson, Robertson-Grosheide.

b. *Lexicons*

(1) For the Old Testament: Gesenius-Buhl (Eng. translation of an earlier edition of Gesenius by Tregelles), Fuerst, Siegfried-Stade, Koenig, Brown, Driver and Briggs.

(2) For the New Testament: Robinson, Thayer, Harting (Dutch), Abbott-Smith, Souter, Cremer (*Biblisch-Theologisches Woerterbuch,* 10th ed. by Koegel, English tr. of fourth ed.), Baljon, *Grieksch-Theologisch Woordenboek.*

c. *Concordances*

(1) For the Old Testament: Fuerst, Mandelkern (both have the Hebrew Text)

(2) For the New Testament: Brueder (based on the Textus Receptus), Moulton and Geden (based on the text of Westcott and Hort). Both have the Greek text.

(3) General: Trommius (Dutch), Cruden, Walker, Strong, Young (all have the English text)

d. *Special works*

(1) On the Old Testament: Driver, *Hebrew Tenses;* Adams, *Sermons in Accents;* Geden, *Introduction to the Hebrew Bible;* Girdlestone, *Old Testament Synonyms;* Kennedy, *Hebrew Synonyms.*

(2) On the New Testament: Burton, *Moods and Tenses;* Simcox, *The Language of the New Testament;* same, *The Writers of the New Testament;* Trench, *New Testament Synonyms;* Dalman, *The Words of Jesus;* same, *Jesus-Joshua;*

T. Walker, *The Teaching of Jesus and the Jewish Teaching of His Age;* Deissmann, *Light from the Ancient East;* same, *Biblical Studies;* Robertson, *The Minister and His Greek New Testament;* Moulton and Milligan, *The Vocabulary of the Greek Testament.*

e. *Commentaries*

(1) On the Old Testament: Calvin's Commentaries; Keil and Delitzsch; Strack and Zoekler; Lange's Commentary; *The International Critical Commentary;* Jamieson, Fausset, and Brown; *Cambridge Bible; Korte Verklaring* (by several authors); and Commentaries on separate books by Delitzsch, Hoedemaker, Spurgeon, Kok, Sikkel, Alexander, Hengstenberg, Greenhill, Henderson, Pusey, Aalders, Young, and Leupold.

(2) On the New Testament: Calvin's Commentaries; Lange's Commentary; Meyer (the latest edition by J. Weiss is really a new work); *The International Critical Commentary;* Zahn; Alford; *Expositor's Greek Testament;* Jamieson, Fausset, and Brown; *Cambridge Bible; Korte Verklaring; Kommentaar op het Nieuwe Testament,* by Grosheide, Greydanus and others (Bottenburg edition); Erdman, Lenski; Barnes' Notes; and Commentaries on separate books by Ellicott, Lightfoot, Eadie, Brown, Stuart, Westcott, Swete, Mayor, Lindsay, Owen, Beckwith, Godet, Van Andel, Barth, De Moor, and others.

2. THE RIGHT USE OF COMMENTARIES. A few remarks may be appended respecting the proper use of commentaries.

a. In seeking to explain a passage, the interpreter should not immediately resort to the use of commentaries, since this would nip all originality in the bud, involve a great deal of unnecessary labor, and be apt to result in hopeless confusion. He should endeavor first of all to interpret the passage independently, with the aid of whatever internal helps are available, and of such external helps as Grammars, Concordances and Lexicons.

b. If, after making some original study of the passage, he feels the need of consulting one or more commentaries, he ought to avoid the so-called practical commentaries, however good they may be in themselves, for they aim at edification rather than at scientific interpretation.

c. It will greatly facilitate his work, if he approaches the Commentaries, as much as possible, with definite questions in mind. This will be possible only after a certain amount of preliminary original study, but it will save time in that it will obviate the necessity of reading all that the commentaries have to say on the passage under consideration. Moreover, when he comes to the commentaries with a certain line of thought in mind, he will be better prepared to choose between the conflicting opinions which he may encounter.

d. Should he succeed in giving an apparently satisfactory explanation without the aid of commentaries, it will be advisable to compare his interpretation with that given by others. And if he discovers that he goes contrary to the general opinion on some particular point, it will be to the part of wisdom for him to go over the ground carefully once more to see whether he has taken all the data into consideration, and whether his inferences are correct in every particular. He may detect some mistake that will compel him to revise his opinion. But if he finds that every step he took was well warranted, then he should allow his interpretation to stand in spite of all that the commentators may say.

VI. Historical Interpretation

A. Definition and Explanation

This chapter brings us to a new division of Hermeneutics. It is true, Davidson says: "Grammatical and historical interpretation, when rightly understood, are synonymous. The special laws of grammar, agreeably to which the sacred writers employed language, were the result of their peculiar circumstances; and history alone throws us back into those circumstances." But though it is an undoubted fact that the two are closely interwoven and cannot be completely separated, yet it is not only possible, but also highly desirable, to distinguish them and to keep them distinct in our discussion.

Historical interpretation, as here understood, should not be confused with the accommodation theory of Semler, though he dignified it with the same name; nor with the present-day historical-critical method of interpretation, which is based on the philosophy of evolution as applied to history. The term is here used to denote the study of Scripture in the light of those historical circumstances that put their stamp on the different books of the Bible. Immer calls it, "The Real Explanation." In distinction from the grammatical and logical interpretation, which apply to the formal side of Scripture—to the language in which it is couched—the historical refers to the material contents of the Bible. It proceeds on the following assumptions.

1. BASIC ASSUMPTIONS FOR HISTORICAL INTERPRETATION.

a. *The Word of God originated in a historical way, and therefore, can be understood only in the light of history.* This does not mean that everything it contains can be explained historically. As a supernatural revelation of God it naturally harbors elements that transcend the limits of the historical. But it does mean that the contents of the Bible are to a great extent historically determined, and to that extent find their explanation in history.

b. *A word is never fully understood until it is apprehended as a living word, i.e., as it originated in the soul of the author.* Cf. Woltjer, *Het Woord, zijn Oorsprong en Uitlegging,* p. 45. This implies the necessity of what is called the psychological interpretation, which is, in fact, a sub-division of the historical.

c. *It is impossible to understand an author and to interpret his words correctly unless he is seen against the proper historical background.* It is true that a man, in a sense, controls the circumstances of his life, and determines their character; but it is equally true that he is, in a large measure, the product of his historical environment. For example, he is a child of his people, his land, and his age.

d. *The place, the time, the circumstances, and the prevailing view of the world and of life in general, will naturally color the writings that are produced under those conditions of time, place, and circumstances.* This applies also to the books of the Bible, particularly to those that are historical or of an occasional character. In all the range of literature, there is no book that equals the Bible in touching life at every point.

2. DEMANDS ON THE EXEGETE. In view of these presuppositions, historical interpretation makes the following demands on the exegete:

a. *He must seek to know the author whose work he would explain*: his parentage, his character and temperament, his intellectual, moral, and religious characteristics, as well as the external circumstances of his life. He should likewise endeavor to acquaint himself with the speakers that are introduced in the books of the Bible, and with the original readers.

b. *It will be incumbent on him to reconstruct, as far as possible, from the historical data at hand, and with the aid of historical hypotheses, the environment in which the particular writings under consideration originated;* in other words, the author's world. He will have to inform himself respecting the physical features of the land where the books were written, and regarding the character and history, the customs, morals and religion of the people among whom or for whom they were composed.

c. *He will find it to be of the utmost importance that he consider the various influences which determined more directly the character of the writings under consideration,* such as: the original readers, the purpose which the author had in mind, the author's age, his frame of mind, and the special circumstances under which he composed his book.

d. *Moreover, he will have to transfer himself mentally into the first century A.D., and into Oriental conditions.* He must place himself on the standpoint of the author, and seek to enter into his very soul, until he, as it were, lives his life and thinks his thoughts. This means that he will have to guard carefully against the rather common mistake of transferring the author to the present day and making him speak the language of the twentieth century. If he does not avoid this, the danger exists, as McPheeters expresses it, that "the voice he hears (will) be merely the echo of his own ideas" (Bible Student, Vol. III, No. II). His rule should always be that he, "non ex subjecto, sed ex objecto sensum quaerit."

B. Personal Characteristics of the Author or Speaker

1. WHO IS THE AUTHOR? In the historical interpretation of a book, it is natural to ask first of all: Who was its author?

Some of the books of the Bible name their authors; others do not. Hence the query, Who was its author?—even if it is merely considered as a question of a name, is not always easy to answer. But in connection with the historical interpretation of the Bible, the question is far more than that. The mere knowledge of a name does not afford the exegete any material aid. He must seek acquaintance with the author himself: e.g., his character and temperament, his disposition and habitual mode of thought. He should endeavor to penetrate into the secrets of his inner life, in order that he may understand, as far as possible, the motives that control his life, and thus acquire an insight into his thoughts and volitions and actions. It is highly desirable for him to know something about the author's profession, which may have exercised a powerful influence on the man, his manner and his language. The word of Elliott is very much to the point here: "It is sufficient to name the mariner, the soldier, the merchant, the laborer, the clergyman, and the lawyer, in order to call to mind as many different types of men, each having his habitual tone, his familiar expressions, his peculiar images, his favorite point of viewing every subject—in a word, his special nature."

As the best way to get acquainted with others is to associate with them, so the most effective way to become familiar with an author is to study his writings diligently, and to pay particular attention to all personal touches, and to the incidental remarks that bear on his character and life. He who would know Moses, must study the Pentateuch, particularly the last four books, and notice especially such passages as Ex. 2-4; 16:15-19; 33:11; 34:5-7; Numb. 12:7,8; Deut. 34:7-11; Acts 7:20-35; and also Heb. 11:23-29. These shed light on the parentage of the Old Testament mediator, his providential deliverance, his educational advantages, and his ardent love for his people in their distress. Moreover, they clearly portray him as a man who, however impulsive and self-assertive he may have been in his youth, learned humility and patience during a long period of waiting; a man hesitant to venture out on a great undertaking, and yet well qualified for leadership; a man of great intellectual attainments, but of a humble character; a man greatly maligned and abused by his own people, yet loving them with an unselfish and ardent love and bearing their reproaches with exemplary patience—a hero of faith.

In order to know Paul, it will be necessary to read his history as it is recorded by Luke, and also his epistles. Special attention should be paid to such passages as Acts 7:58; 8:1-4; 9:1, 2, 22, 26; 26:9; 13:46-48; Rom. 9:1-3; I Cor. 15:9; II Cor. 11; 12:1-11; Gal. 1:13-15; 2:11-16; Phil. 1:7, 8, 12-18; 3:5-14; I Tim. 1:13-16. In these passages the figure of Paul stands forth as a product, partly of the diaspora and partly of the rabbinical school of Gamaliel, a man thoroughly versed in Jewish literature, having the courage of his convictions; a conscientious persecutor of the Church, but also a truly penitent convert, willing to confess the error of his way; a loyal servant of Jesus Christ, anxious to spend himself in the service of his Lord; yearning for the salvation of his kinsmen, but also praying and working with indefatigable zeal and with indomitable courage for the saving of the Gentiles; a man quite willing to deny himself that God in Christ might receive all the glory.

An intimate acquaintance with the author of a book will facilitate the proper understanding of his words. It will enable the interpreter to surmise, and, perhaps, to establish conclusively, how the words and expressions were born within the soul of the writer; will illumine certain phrases and sentences in an unexpected way, and make them seem more real as the embodiments of living force. Jeremiah stands before us in the Bible as a sensitive, tender-hearted, and impulsive character, who indeed shrinks from the performance of his duty. This knowledge will aid the interpreter in understanding the tenderness and pathetic beauty that characterizes parts of his writings, and also to appreciate his passionate anger in rebuking the enemy (11:20; 12:3; 15:10 ff; 17:15-18); his complaint that the Lord does not reveal the power of his arm, and his cursing the day of his birth (20:7-18) . . . The apostle John was evidently by nature an impetuous and vehement character, occasionally swayed by selfish ambition, and so zealous in the work of the Lord that he became severe on those whom he regarded as unfair competitors and enemies of Jesus. But the natural defects of his character were chastened by grace. His love was sanctified, his zeal led in proper channels. He drank deeply at the fountain of life, and reflected more than others on the mysteries of the wonderful life of the Saviour. This explains to a great extent the difference between his Gospel and the Synoptics, and also accounts for the fact that he stresses the necessity of abiding in Christ and of love to Christ and the brethren . . . In reading the prophecy of Amos, it will be helpful to bear in mind the simple fact that he was a herdsman of Tekoa, which will account for many of his figurative expressions. Ezekiel would hardly have written as he did in chapters 40-48 of his prophecy, if he had not been one of the exilic priests, thoroughly acquainted with the temple ritual and mindful of the fact that Zion's past glory had departed.

2. WHO IS THE SPEAKER? Another question that comes up under this heading is, "Who is the speaker?" The Biblical authors often introduce others as speakers, and it is of the utmost importance that the expositor should carefully distinguish between the words of the author himself and those of the speaker or speakers that are introduced. In the historical

books, the line of demarcation is generally so clear that it is not easily overlooked. Yet there are exceptions. For example, it is rather difficult to determine whether the words found in John 3:16-21 were spoken by Jesus to Nicodemus, or form an explanatory addition added by John. In the prophets, the sudden transitions from the human to the divine are, as a rule, easily recognized by the change from the third to the first person, in connection with the character of what is said. Cf. Hosea 9:9, 10; Zech. 12:8-10; 14:1-3. Sometimes a dialogue is found between the writer and a supposed opponent. Such cases require careful handling, for failure to distinguish correctly is very apt to result in serious mistakes. Cf. Mal. 3:13-16; Rom. 3:1-9. The following rule will prove to be of some value: *"The writer of the book should be regarded as the speaker until some express evidence to the contrary appears."* And when the interpreter knows who the speaker, as distinguished from the writer, is, he should make it a point to increase his knowledge of him with all the means at his command. Such persons as Abraham, Isaac, Jacob, Joseph, Samuel, Job and his friends, and such classes of persons as the Pharisees, the Sadducees, and the Scribes, must be made the objects of special study. The better they are known, the better their words will be understood.

EXERCISE: Read the following Psalms in the light of David's character and experiences: Ps. 23, 24, 32, 51, 72, 132. How did Hosea's character and personal history determine the character of his prophecy? In what respect is the individuality of Paul, Peter, and James stamped on their respective writings? Who is the speaker in Isa. 53; Hosea 5 and 6; Hab. 2; Ps. 2, 22; and 40?

C. Social Circumstances of the Author

The social circumstances comprehend all those that are not peculiar to the author, but which he shares with his contemporaries. They are naturally of a rather general character.

1. Geographical Circumstances. Climatic and geographical circumstances in general often influence the thought, the language, and the representations of a writer, and leave an imprint on his literary productions. Hence, the interpreter of the Bible should have special acquaintance with the geography of the Holy Land, the native country of the Biblical authors. It is of importance for him to understand the character of the seasons, the prevailing winds and their function, and the difference of temperature in the valleys, on the highlands and on the mountain-tops. He should have some knowledge of the productions of the land: of its trees and shrubs and flowers, its grains and vegetables and fruits, its animals, both wild and domesticated, its indigenous insects and its native birds. Mountains and valleys, lakes and rivers, cities and villages, highways and plains—he must be acquainted with them and their location.

For the study of the permanent features of the Holy Land, such works as Robinson's *Biblical Researches,* Thomson's *The Land and the Book,* Stanley's *Sinai and Palestine,* and G. A. Smith's *Historical Geography of the Holy Land,* have the greatest value. But for an inquiry into that which is more variable, such as the fruitfulness of the soil, the location of cities and villages, etc., earlier works, such as those of Josephus and Eusebius (Onomasticon) are to be preferred. This study is essential particularly in view of the fact that Orientals generally lived very close to nature, saw it instinct with life, and had an open eye for its symbolism. The discourses and parables of the Saviour, for example, are replete with striking passages in which the symbolic relation between the natural and the spiritual is indicated. He compares the Kingdom of God to a grain of mustard seed (Matt. 13:31, 32), and likens Israel to a fig tree (Luke 13:6-9). He speaks of himself as the true vine and of his Father as the husbandman (John 15:1).

It is quite evident, and therefore needs no elaborate proof, that the expositor should be acquainted with the physical features of Palestine, its climate, topography, productions, etc. How can he explain the poet's statement that the "dew of Hermon descended on the mountains of Zion" (Ps. 133:3), unless he is familiar with the effect of Hermon's snow-clad peak on the mists that are constantly arising from the ravines at its foot? How shall he interpret such expressions as "the glory of Lebanon" and "the excellency of Carmel and Sharon," if he has no knowledge of their luxuriant vegetation and surpassing beauty? What can he say in explanation of the use of chariots in the Northern kingdom (I Kings 18:44 ff.; 22:29 ff.; II Kings 5:9 ff.; 9:16; 10:12, 15), and their absence from the Southern kingdom? How can he account for the success of David in eluding Saul, though they came within speaking distance of each other, unless he understands the character of the country? Only familiarity with the seasons will enable him to interpret such passages as Cant. 2:11, "For, lo, the winter is past, the rain is over and gone"; and Matt. 24:20, "But pray that your flight be not in the winter."

2. POLITICAL CIRCUMSTANCES. The political condition of a people also leaves a profound impression upon its national literature. The Bible contains ample evidence of this also, and therefore it is quite necessary that the expositor should inform himself respecting the political organization of the nations that play an important part in it. Their national history, their relations with other nations, and their political institutions should be made the object of careful study. Particular attention must be devoted to the political changes in the national life of Israel.

History only sheds light on the question of why Israel was not permitted to distress the Moabites and Ammonites (cf. Deut. 2:9, 19). The dependent position of Edom in the days of Solomon and Jehoshaphat explains how these kings could build a navy of ships at Ezion-giber, in the land of Edom (1 Kings 9:26; 22:47, 48; I Chron. 18:13; II Chron. 8:17, 18). Such passages as II Kings 15:19; 16:7; Isa. 20:1 find their explanation in the rising power of the Assyrians and the gradual extension of their empire, as revealed especially by the inscriptions of their kings. The words of Rabshakeh in II Kings 18:21 and Isa. 36:6 become luminous in view of the fact that there was a rather influential Egyptian party in Judah during the reign of Hezekiah (Isa. 30:1-7). The radical change in the political position and constitution of Israel must be borne in mind in the interpretation of the post-exilic writings. Such passages as Ezra 4:4-6 ff.; Neh. 5:14, 15; Zech. 7:3-5; 8:19; Mal. 1:8, can only be explained in the light of contemporary history. And on turning from the Old Testament to the New, the interpreter encounters a situation for which he is entirely unprepared, unless he has made a study of the inter-testamentary period. The Romans are the dominant power, and Idumaeans have rule over the heritage of Jacob. Parties that were never heard of in the Old Testament now occupy the center of the stage. There is a Jewish Sanhedrin that decides matters of the greatest importance, and a class of scribes that has practically supplanted the priests as teachers of the people. Hence, all kinds of questions arise. How was the Jewish state constituted? By what irony of history did Idumaeans become the recognized rulers of the Jewish people? What limitations did the Roman supremacy impose on the Jewish government? Did the existing parties have political significance; and if so, what did they aim at? A study of Israel's past will give answer to these questions. Such passages as Matt. 2:22, 23; 17:24-27; 22:16-21; 27:2; John 4:9, can only be explained in the light of history.

3. RELIGIOUS CIRCUMSTANCES. The religious life of Israel did not always move on the same plane, was not always characterized by true spirituality. There were seasons of spiritual elevation, but these were soon followed by periods of moral and religious degradation. The generations that served God with a humble and reverent spirit were repeatedly succeeded by such as worshipped idol-gods, or sought satisfaction in hypocritical lip-service. The history of Israel's religion, when viewed as a whole, reveals deterioration rather than progress, devolution instead of evolution.

The period of the Judges was one of a religious syncretism that resulted from the fusion of the service of Jehovah with the worship of the Canaanitish Baalim. In the days of Samuel, the prophetic order began to assert itself and exercised a beneficial influence on the spiritual life of the nation. The period of the Kings was characterized in Judah by repeated declines and revivals. Worship on high places and, at times, even flagrant idolatry, was the besetting sin of the people. During the same period, the typical sin of the Northern kingdom was its calf-worship, augmented in the days of Ahab by the worship of Melkart, the Phoenician Baal. After the exile, idolatry was rare in Israel, but its religion degenerated into cold formalism and dead orthodoxy.

These things must be taken into consideration in the interpretation of those passages that refer to the religious life of the people. Moreover, the interpreter should be acquainted with the religious institutions and practices of Israel, as regulated by the Mosaic law. Such passages as Judg. 8:28, 33; 10:6; 17:6, can only be explained in the light of contemporary history. In I Sam. 2:13-17, the writer himself gives a historical explanation of the manner in which the sons of Eli disregarded the law. The question of why Jeroboam set up calves at Dan and Bethel can only be answered historically. History gives answer to the question as to why the pious kings and prophets of Judah are constantly combating the worship on high places, while the prophets of Ephraim seldom condemn this practice. Without the necessary historical knowledge, the expositor will find it impossible to understand the word of the angel to Manoah, "the child shall be a nazarite to God" (Judg.13:7); Jeremiah's reference to the valley of Hinnom as "the valley of slaughter" (Jer. 19:6; comp. 7:31-33); Micah's mention of "the statutes of Omri" (Micah 6:16); Jesus' injunction to the leper to go and show himself to the priest (Matt. 8:4); and his reference to "the ministrels and the people making a noise" (Matt. 9:23); and to those that "sold oxen and sheep and doves, and the changers of money" (John 2:14). It is history that will enable him to explain such expressions as, "we are buried with him by baptism unto death" (Rom. 6:4); and, "For even Christ our Passover is sacrificed for us." The great significance of historical knowledge is brought to him when he encounters a passage like I Cor. 15:29, referring, as it does, to a custom of which we have no certain knowledge.

D. Circumstances Peculiar to the Writings

Besides the general circumstances of the author's life, there are some of a more special character that influenced his writings directly. Sound interpretation requires, of course, that they especially be taken into consideration.

1. THE ORIGINAL READERS AND HEARERS. For the correct understanding of a writing or discourse, it is of the utmost importance to know for whom it was first of all intended. This applies particularly to those books of the Bible that are of an occasional character, such as the prophetical books

and the New Testament Epistles. These were naturally adapted to the special circumstances and the particular needs of the reader. The writer of necessity took into account their geographical, historical, and social position, their industrial and commercial relations, their educational and social advantages, their moral and religious character, and their personal idiosyncrasies, prejudices, and peculiar habits of thought. And his knowledge of these is reflected in his book. This accounts to a great extent for the characteristic differences of the Synoptic Gospels. The defection of the Galatians accounts for the severity of the Epistle which Paul wrote to them. And the unselfish devotion of the Philippians to the great apostle of the Gentiles, and their adherence to his doctrine, explain the fundamental note of gratitude and joy that marks the letter which they received from Paul, the prisoner.

The condition of the original readers not only determines the general character of the writing, but also explains many of its particulars. The divisions at Corinth clearly gave Paul occasion to say: "For all things are yours; whether Paul, or Apollos, or Cephas . . . all are yours; and ye are Christ's, and Christ is God's" (I Cor. 3:20-23). And where the apostle says in I Cor. 15:32, "If after the manner of men I have fought with the beasts at Ephesus," it is not at all unlikely that the form of expression was suggested by the fact that such fights were rather common at Corinth. Does not the condition of the Galatian church explain why Paul, who himself circumcised Timothy, should write to them: "Behold, I Paul say unto you that, if ye be circumcised, Christ shall profit you nothing" (Gal. 5:2). Why should he write to the Colossians rather than to others: "For in him dwelleth all the fulness of the godhead bodily" (Col. 2:9). An intimate knowledge of the original readers will often illumine the pages of a writing addressed to them in an unexpected and striking manner. The same principle applies to the original hearers of a discourse, so that they, too, should be made the object of special study.

2. THE PURPOSE OF THE AUTHOR. The writers of the Biblical books naturally had some purpose in mind in their production; and the interpreter should make it his business to keep this purpose steadily in mind. We may believe that the mind of the writer was constantly fixed on it, and that he was guided by it in the selection of his material and in the expression of his thoughts. Therefore the knowledge of the end he had in mind will not only aid in understanding the book as a whole, but will also illumine the details. Elliott correctly remarks: "This object once discovered will complete the abridged phrases, throw light upon obscurities, and detect the true meaning when several interpretations are possible. The object will aid in distinguishing the literal from the figurative, the relative from the absolute, and the main from the secondary thoughts" (*Biblical Hermeneutics*, p. 166).

It is not always easy to determine the object of a writing. In some cases the interpreter will have to depend upon an ecclesiastical tradition that is not always reliable, but should be received with reserve. In others the author himself states the purpose of his book, as Solomon, in Prov. 1:2-4; Luke, in 1:1-4; John, in John 20:31, and Rev. 1:1; Peter, in I Pet. 5:12. In still others the knowledge of the original readers and the circumstances in which they lived together with the occasion that led to the composition of a book will aid in the discovery of its purpose, as I Corinthians, I Thessalonians, and Hebrews. But there are also instances in which only the repeated reading of a book will help one to detect its object. Certain recurring expressions or remarks will often betray it. The tenfold *eleh toledoth* (these are the generations) in Genesis (cf. 2:4; 5:1; 6:9; 10:1; 11:10; 11:27; 25:19; 36:1; 37:2) points to it as the book of births or beginnings. The repeated references in the Gospel of John to the way in which the disciples were led to believe in Christ, and to the unbelief of others, points to the object of the Gospel (cf. 2:11; 6:64, 68; 7:38; 12:16; 14:1; 16:31; 17:8; 20:29). Similarly the judgment that is passed on the kings of Israel and Judah at their death, points to the fact that the books of Kings were written to bring out how little the political leaders of the people, and consequently also the people themselves, measured up to the divine standard.

3. THE TIME OF LIFE, THE SPECIAL CIRCUMSTANCES, AND FRAME OF MIND, in which the author wrote his work, are important considerations. While we should guard against the extreme of some irreverent Rationalists who claim that John evidently wrote his first Epistle, when he was too old to think clearly and logically, we should bear in mind that the Spirit of God employed the sacred writers in an organic way, and did not cause a young man to write like one who had lived to a ripe old age, nor an old man, like one in the prime of life. It is but natural that the literary productions of those who have not yet crossed the meridian of life, should be characterized by originality and virility; and the writings of those who have passed on to their declining years, by a serious outlook on life and practical wisdom. Compare Galatians with II Timothy, and Peter's speeches in the Acts of the Apostles with his Second Epistle. Study also the farewell discourse of Moses (Deut. 31, 32) and the last words of David (II Sam. 23:1-7).

The author's historical circumstances and his frame of mind also influenced his writing. This applies, not only to the books of the Bible, but also to the speeches and discourses that are recorded in it. It is impossible to interpret the touching elegy of David on the occasion of Saul and Jonathan's death, except in the light of his profound reverence for the anointed of the Lord, and of his great love for Jonathan (II Sam. 1:19-

27). How shall anyone give an adequate explanation of the Lamentations of Jeremiah, unless he is acquainted with the sad plight of the Holy City, and with the dejection and anguish of the disconsolate prophet? The real sentiment and the touching beauty of the 137th Psalm can only be understood by him who realizes the great attachment of the pious exiles to Jerusalem, and the wistful longings for Zion that filled their heart. Cf. also John 14:16; Phil. 1:12-35; II Tim. 4:6-18.

But while the interpreter should gratefully apply whatever historical knowledge he has at his command, in the interpretation of the Bible, he must be careful not to let his imagination run riot in the exposition of Scripture. What is purely the fruit of the imagination should never be presented as historical truth.

E. Helps for the Historical Interpretation

1. INTERNAL. The principal resources for the historical interpretation of Scripture are found in the Bible itself. In distinction from all other writings, it contains the absolute truth, and therefore its information deserves to be preferred to that gleaned from other sources. This reminder is not superfluous in view of the fact that many seem inclined to give more credence to the voices of hoary antiquity that were made vocal by recent archaeological discoveries than to the infallible Word of God. The believing and conscientious expositor will ask first of all: What does the Bible say?

In II Chron. 30:1, King Hezekiah commands all Israel and Judah to keep the Passover. If the interpreter desires more light on this feast, he should not turn to Josephus in the first place, but to such passages of Scripture as Ex. 12:1-21; Lev. 23:4-14; Num. 28:16 ff.; Deut. 16:1-8. According to the prophecy of the angel to Manoah, Samson was destined to be a nazarite (Judg. 13:5). But what was a nazarite? The

answer to that question is found in Num. 6. Zephaniah pro-
nounces judgment on those "that swear by Malcham." I
Kings 11:5, 7, 33 speak of him as the god of the Ammonites,
and Lev. 18:21 and 20:2-5 point to the fact that he was
served with human sacrifices. In the New Testament we
meet with the party of the Sadducees, and the question
arises, What characterized them? The following passages
give at least a partial answer to that query: Matt. 22:23;
Mark 12:18; Luke 20:27; Acts 23:8. The Samaritans are
repeatedly named also, and again we ask, Who were they?
The study of such passages as II Kings 17:24-41; Ezra 4, and
Nehemiah 4 enlighten us.

2. EXTERNAL. If the expositor has exhausted the resources
of Scripture and still needs further information, he should turn
to the profane sources at his command.

a. *The inscriptions.* These are undoubtedly very important.
They disclose to the world the history of comparatively unknown periods, and often serve to correct erroneous historical
accounts. Hence it would be unwarranted for the interpreter to disregard the information which they convey.

(1) *For the Old Testament.* The cuneiform inscriptions
are of the greatest importance: the accounts of the creation
and the flood, the Tel-el-Amarna Tablets, the Code of Ham-
murabi, and the inscriptions of the great Assyrian and Baby-
lonian kings. Yet they should not be regarded as absolutely
reliable from a historical point of view. For example, it
is generally admitted at present that the accounts of the kings
are exaggerated and aim at the aggranizement or glorifi-
cation of these monarchs rather than at historical truth. The
works of H. Winckler and E. Schrader contain valuable col-
lections of these inscriptions as they bear on the contents of
the Old Testament. The following works in the English language are also valuable: Barton, *Archaeology and the Bible;*

Naville, *Archaeology and the Old Testament*: Price, *The Monuments and the Old Testament*: Bliss, *The Development of the Palestine Exploration;* Kenyon, *The Bible and Archaeology; Noordtzij, Gods Woord en der Feuwen Getuigenis;* Van Deursem, *Het Land van den Bijbel;* Baarslag, *De Bijbelsche Geschiedenis in de Omlijsting van het Oosten.*

(2) *For the New Testament.* Here the inscriptions on the Egyptian papyri and ostraca, and those found in Asia Minor are of primary significance. The former, however, have linquistic rather than historical value, though they are not devoid of historical interest; while the latter bear on the history more than on the language of the New Testament. The following are some of the most important works that are easily accessible: Deissmann. *Light from the Ancient East;* ibid., *Biblical Studies;* Ramsay's works, especially, *The Bearing of Recent Discovery on the Trustworthiness of the New Testament;* Cobern, *The New Archaeological Discoveries and their Bearing upon the New Testament;* Kenyon, *The Bible and the Ancient Manuscripts.*

b. *Other historical writings.* Among these, the works of Josephus, viz., his *Antiquities of the Jews,* and *Jewish War,* deserve the place of honor. The first ten books of his *Antiquities* contain very little that is not also contained in the Old Testament. The real value of his greatest work begins with the 11th book. From that book on, the author refers to many sources that are not accessible now, such as Berosus, Nicholas of Damascus, Alexander Polyhistor, Menander, and others. Naturally, the value of this part of his work depends largely on the sources which he employed. It is evident that he used them more or less critically, but it is not absolutely certain that his evaluation of them is correct. Josephus is often accused of subjectivity and of historical inaccuracy. Yet it would seem that, on the whole, his work is perfectly reliable, though it must be admitted that in the apologetic part of his work he flatters the Jews somewhat. His *Jewish War* is regarded as a reliable and very valuable work. The only objection to it is that the numbers are often exaggerated, and that the heroic deeds and the magnanimity of the Romans receive undue praise.

The History of Herodotus is valuable for the study of the Persian period. But even according to the testimony of his most moderate critics, he is not always reliable, and must be used with caution.

Furthermore, the Talmud and the writings of the Rabbis may serve to elucidate the historical portion of the Bible. Lightfoot gathered an important collection of Jewish sayings that bear on the contents of Scripture, in his *Horae Hebraicae et Talmudicae*.

It is possible that the expositor, in studying these sources, will occasionally find that they apparently conflict with the Bible. In such cases, he should not hastily conclude that Scripture is mistaken, but must always bear in mind that, while there may be error of transcription, the Bible is the infallible Word of God. It may be that our extra-biblical sources are not reliable at the point in question, or that they merely conflict with an erroneous interpretation of a Scriptural passage. Therefore, whenever he encounters cases of apparent conflict, he will have to investigate the veracity of these profane sources; and if this is found to be above reasonable doubt, he may have to revise his exegetical views, but it is also possible that he may meet with an insoluble difficulty; that an apparently reliable source conflicts, not with his interpretation of the Bible, but, as far as he can see, with the Bible itself. In such cases there is only one legitimate course, viz., to cling faithfully to the statement of the Bible, and to wait patiently for additional light. It is not at all impossible, as the cases of Sargon and Belshazzar prove, that a seemingly reliable source may in the end prove untrustworthy.

EXERCISE: Explain the following passages historically, i. e., in the light of geographical, political, or religious circumstances, or from the point of view of the object of a book, the environment of the author, his age or frame of mind: Gen. 23:3-16; Deut. 32:11; I Sam. 15:2, 3; II Sam. 21:1-6; II Kings 17:4; Ezra 7:21; Neh. 2:10, 19; Esther 3:8; Ps. 2:6; 9:14; 11:1; 22:16; 29:3-9; 63:1; 99:1; 125:1, 2; Prov. 29:23; Cant. 4:16; Isa. 3:16; 20:1; Hosea 7:11; 10:5; Joel 1:9; 2:20, 23; Micah 3:5-8; Matt. 1:19; 5:20; 23:37, 38; Luke 2:1-3; 13:1 John 1:21; I Cor. 10:21; Gal. 3:3; Col. 2:16-18; II Tim. 4:6-8.

LITERATURE: Davidson, *Sacred Hermeneutics,* pp. 320-333; Terry, *Biblical Hermeneutics,* pp. 129-140; Lutz, *Biblische Hermeneutik,* pp. 228-274; Immer, *Hermeneutics,* pp. 259-330.

VII. Theological Interpretation

A. Name

Many writers on Hermeneutics are of the opinion that the grammatical and historical interpretation meet all the requirements for the proper interpretation of the Bible. They have no eye for the special theological character of this discipline. There are others, however, who are conscious of the necessity of recognizing a third element in the interpretation of Scripture. Kuyper emphasizes the necessity of recognizing the *mystical* factor in the interpretation of Scripture (*Theol. Enc.* III, p. 101 vv.), and Bavinck insists that the Bible be read *theologically* (*Dogm.* I, p. 471). Klausen and Landerer speaks of *theological,* and Cellerier and Sikkel, of a *scriptural interpretation.* They all agree in the desire to do justice to the special theological element of the Bible, and refuse to place it on a level with other books.

Scripture contains a great deal that does not find its explanation in history, nor in the secondary authors, but only in God as the *Auctor primarius.* Purely historical and psychological considerations will not account for the following facts: (1) that the Bible is the Word of God; (2) that it constitutes an organic whole, of which each individual book is an integral part; (3) that the Old and New Testament are related to each other as type and antitype, prophecy and fulfilment, germ and perfect development; and (4) that not only the explicit statements of the Bible, but also what may be deduced from it by good and necessary consequence, constitutes the Word of God. In view of all this, it is not only perfectly warranted, but absolutely necessary, to complement the usual grammatical and historical interpretation with a third.

The name "Theological Interpretation" deserves the preference, as expressive, at once, of the fact that its necessity follows from the divine authorship of the Bible, and of the equally important consideration that, in the last analysis, God is the proper Interpreter of His Word. The following subjects call for discussion: (1) The interpretation of the Bible as a unity; (2) The mystical sense of Scripture; (3) The implications of the Bible; and (4) Helps for the theological interpretation.

B. The Bible as a Unity

1. THE RELATION OF THE OLD TESTAMENT TO THE NEW. In view of the present-day tendency to emphasize the diversity of the contents of the Bible, it is not superfluous to call particular attention to the fact that it should be interpreted as a unity. And the first question that confronts the interpreter is that of the relation in which the Old and the New Testaments stand to each other. Past history revealed two opposite views that asserted and re-asserted themselves repeatedly in various forms. There was the antinomian error of ascribing too much of the carnal element to Judaism, on the one hand; and on the other, the nomistic fallacy of imposing too much of the Judaistic on Christianity. The one elevated the Christian at the expense of the Jewish religion, to which it ascribed a purely national, external, and temporal character; and in so doing, fostered the idea that the Old Testament has no permanent validity. The other conceived of the New Testament as a *nova lex,* somewhat on the order of the Old Testament, and in course of time led to the institution of a separate priesthood, the erection of altars on which sacrifices were again brought, and the consecration of sacred times and places.

In opposition to these views, it is necessary to emphasize the unity of the Bible. Both the Old and the New Testament form essential parts of God's special revelation. God is the Author of both, and in both has the same purpose in mind. They both contain the same doctrine of redemption, preach the same Christ, and impose upon men the same moral and religious duties. At the same time, the revelation they contain is progressive, and gradually increases in definiteness, clearness, and spiritual conception. As the New Testament is implicit in the Old, so the Old is explicit in the New. Therefore we say that

a. *The Old and New Testament constitute a unit.*

(1) *The doctrine of redemption was essentially the same for those who lived under the old covenant as it is for the Church of the New Testament.* This is sometimes forgotten by those who, while recognizing the typical element of the Old Testament, lose sight of the symbolical character of many of its institutions and ceremonies. They see in the ceremonial institutions, rites and transactions of the Old Testament, only external forms that had no spiritual significance, and bodily exercises that profited but little; while in fact these ceremonies were symbols of spiritual truths. The sacrifices that were brought spoke of the forgiveness of sin on the basis of the atoning blood of Christ, and the oft-repeated washings symbolized the purifying influence of the Holy Spirit. The tabernacle as a whole was a revelation of the way that led to God, and Canaan itself constituted a symbol of the rest that remains for the people of God. The following passages prove that the Israelites had some conceptions of the spiritual significance of their rites and ceremonies: Lev. 26:41; 20:25, 26; Ps. 26:6; 51:7, 16, 17; Isa. 1:16.

(2) *The true Israelites in the Old Testament, as well as in the New, are not the natural descendants of Abraham as such,*

but only they who share his faith. In the election of Israel,
God did not, in the last analysis, aim at the separation of Israel
as a nation, but at the formation of a spiritual people, primarily gathered out of the chosen race, but also in part out of the
surrounding nations. From the earliest times, proselytes were
incorporated into Israel. Solomon, in his dedicatory prayer,
did not forget the stranger who might come to worship in the
temple (I Kings 8:41 ff.) ; and the prophets looked forward
with joyful expectancy to the time when the Gentiles, too,
would bring their treasures into the temple of the Lord.

(3) *The difference between the privileges and duties of the
Old and of the New Testament people of God was purely relative, and not absolute.* It is true, the Old Testament and the
New are occasionally contrasted in the Bible. This is possible
in view of the fact that the one emphasizes the law, and the
other, grace. But there is no absolute antithesis. Even in the
Old Testament the law was subservient to the covenant of
grace. It was not purely an external rule; the pious Israelite
had it written on the tablets of his heart (Ps. 37:31; 40:8).
They were not saved in any other way than New Testament
believers. They needed the same Mediator and the same Holy
Spirit, and received the same blessings of the covenant of
grace, though not so abundantly, nor in exactly the same manner. The Old and the New Testament are related to each
other not merely as type and antitype, but also as bud and
flower, as a primitive and a more perfect revelation.

(4) *The ordinances of the old and new covenants are distinguished only by relative differences, such as correspond in
nature to the change in the divine economy, and in the spiritual
condition of those placed under it.* In the Old Testament,
circumcision and passover, sacrifices and purifications were
not simply carnal institutions pertaining to the flesh, mere
shadows of a coming reality. They also pertained to the con-

science; and acceptable participation in them required faith on the part of the worshipper. It is quite true that, as the Epistle to the Hebrews says, "they could not make him that did the service perfect, as pertaining to the conscience" (Heb. 9:9). But this does not imply that they concerned only the purification of the flesh. Such purification would have had no meaning for one who was guilty of fraud, oppression, deceit, and the swearing of a false oath. Yet forgiveness for such sins was attainable through the appointed offerings. They had spiritual significance, as well as baptism and the Lord's Supper have in the New Testament dispensation, but of course, only in connection with the coming perfect sacrifice of Jesus Christ.

b. *In the interpretation of the Old and the New Testaments in their mutual relation, the interpreter should be guided by definite considerations.*

(1) *The Old Testament offers the key to the right interpretation of the New.* The contents of the New Testament are already the fruit of a long previous development. The Old Testament, for instance, contains the account of creation and of man's fall in sin, of the establishment of the covenant of grace and of the adumbrations of the coming Redeemer. All these are presupposed in the New Testament, and knowledge of them is a prerequisite for its proper understanding. Moreover, the Old Testament contains a great deal that serves to illustrate New Testament passages. Cf. John 3:14, 15; Rom. 4:9-13; Heb. 13:10-13.

(2) *The New Testament is a commentary on the Old.* While the Old Testament contains but a shadowy representation of spiritual realities, the New Testament presents them in the perfect light of the fulness of time. The one contains types, the other antitypes; the one, prophecy, the other, fulfilment. The more perfect revelation of the New Testament illumines the

pages of the Old.   Sometimes New Testament writers furnish explicit and striking explanations of Old Testament passages, and reveal depths that might easily have escaped the interpreter.   Cf. Acts 2:29-31; Matt. 11:10; 21:42; Gal. 4:22-
31; and the whole Epistle to the Hebrews.

(3) On the one hand, *the interpreter should beware of mini-
mizing the Old Testament.* This was the mistake of those who
had a too carnal conception of Israel and its religious institutions, and of the privileges and duties of the Old Testament
people of God.   It is the error of many in the present day, who
regard the Old Testament simply as the fruit of historical development, and who, in some cases, boldly declare that it has
had its day now that the New Testament is in our possession.

(4) On the other hand, *he should guard against reading too
much into the Old Testament.* This is done, for instance,
whenever the details of the work of redemption, as revealed
in the New Testament, are read back into the Old Testament.
Many interpreters, for instance, find in Gen. 3:15 already the
promise of a *personal* Redeemer.   The great question for the
exegete is, how much God actually revealed in any particular
passage.   This can only be determined by a careful study of
the passage in question, in its proper context, and in connection with the exact stage of God's progressive revelation to
which it belongs.

2. The Significance of the Different Books of the
Bible in the Organism of Scripture.

a. *General Considerations.* The Word of God is an organic
production, and consequently the separate books that constitute it are organically related to one another.   The Holy Spirit
so directed the human authors in writing the books of the Bible
that their productions are mutually complementary.   They are
one in recording the work which God, in the execution of his
divine plan, wrought in Christ for the redemption of a peo-

ple that would glorify him eternally. The Old Testament reveals this work, first of all, historically in the formation and guidance of Israel as a nation. The poetical books and the wisdom literature disclose its fruit in the spiritual experiences and the practical life of God's people. And the prophets view it in the light of God's eternal council, emphasizing the failure of the people to live up to the divine requirements, and directing the hopes of the pious to the future. A similar line of development runs through the New Testament. The Gospels and Acts contain the history of the work of redemption in Christ. The Epistles reveal the effect of this work in the life and experience of the churches. And the Apocalypse discloses its final issue in rays of heavenly light.

b. *Specific Examples.* These general considerations lead on to the question, *How is each book related to the Bible as a whole?* The answer to this query can be found only by a careful study of the books in connection with the leading ideas of Scripture. The interpreter should make it his aim to discover, not merely what message each book contained for the contemporaries of the authors, but what permanent value it has, what word of God it conveys to all following generations. For the sake of illustration, we add the leading ideas of some of the books of the Bible. Genesis speaks to all ages until the end of time, of the creation of man in the image of God; of the entrance of sin into the world; and of the initial revelation of God's redeeming grace. Exodus acquaints the successive generations of men with the doctrine of deliverance through the shedding of blood, while Leviticus teaches them how sinful man can approach God and stand in his holy presence. Numbers pictures the pilgrimage of God's people, and Deuteronomy points to the blessing that accompanies a life of obedience to God and to the curse that awaits the unfaithful. The book of Job offers a solution for the problem of suffering in the life of God's people; the Psalms furnish an insight into the spiritual experiences of the people of God—their struggles and triumphs, their joy and sorrow. If Isaiah describes the love of God for his people, Jeremiah offers a revelation of his righteousness. While Ezekiel emphasizes the holiness of the Lord, who would sanctify his Name among the nations, Daniel reveals the glory of the Lord, as exalted above all the kings of the earth. In the Epistle to the Galatians, Paul defends the liberty of the people of God as over against the ceremonialism of the Old Testament. And while, in his letter to the Ephesians, he calls attention to the unity of the Church, in that to the Colossians he magnifies Christ as the head of the Church.

If the interpreter studies the books of the Bible with such leading ideas in mind, this will greatly aid him to see, for instance, that Paul and James do not teach conflicting doctrines, but simply view the same truth from different aspects, and are therefore mutually complementary.

C. The Mystical Sense of Scripture

The study of the mystical sense of Scripture has not always been characterized by the necessary caution. Some expositors have defended the untenable position that every part of the Bible has besides its literal, also a mystical sense. Others recoiled from that unwarranted position, and went to the extreme of denying outright the existence of any mystical sense. More careful scholars, however, preferred to take the middle ground that certain parts of Scripture have a mystical sense which, in such cases, does not constitute a second, but the real sense of the Word of God. The necessity of recognizing the mystical sense is quite evident from the way in which the New Testament often interprets the Old. The works of Turpie, *The New Testament View of the Old,* and, *The Old Testament in the New,* and those of J. Scott. *Principles of New*

Testament Quotation and F. Johnson, *The Quotations of the New Testament from the Old,* are instructive in this respect.

1. GUIDES TO DISCOVERY OF THE MYSTICAL SENSE. Dr. Kuyper says that the interpreter, in his attempt to discover the mystical sense, should bear in mind that:

a. *Scripture itself contains indications of a mystical sense.* For example, it is well known that the New Testament interprets several passages of the Old Testament messianically, and in so doing, not only points to the presence of the mystical sense, in those particular passages, but also intimates that whole categories of related passages should be interpreted in a similar manner.

b. *A symbolical relation exists between the different spheres of life, in virtue of the fact that all life is organically related.* The natural world is symbolically related to the spiritual: the life that now is, to the veiled glories of the life to come. Thus Paul in Ephesians 5, points to marriage as a mystery indicative of the relation between Christ and the Church.

c. *History is characterized by dioramatic unity, in virtue of which analogous events often re-appear, though it be with slight modifications, and these repetitions are, more or less, typically related.* Israel was a typical people, and the history of that ancient people of God is rich in typical elements. This is clearly proved by many Old Testament quotations in the New, by such passages as Gal. 4:22-31, and by the entire Epistle to the Hebrews.

d. *A close connection between the individual and communal life clearly reveals itself in lyric poetry.* In the lyric psalms, the sacred poets do not sing as detached individuals, but as members of the community. They share the joy and sorrow of the people of God, which is, in the last analysis, the joy and sorrow of Him in whom the Church finds its bond of union. This is evident from the psalms in which we listen alternately to the poet, the community, and the Messiah.

2. EXTENT OF THE MYSTICAL SENSE. The mystical sense of the Bible is not limited to any one book of the Bible, nor to any one of the fundamental forms of God's revelation, as, for example, prophecy. It is found in several biblical writings, and in the historical and poetical, as well as in the prophetical books. Its character can best be brought out in a brief discussion of: (1) The Symbolical and Typical Interpretation of Scripture; (2) The Interpretation of Prophecy; (3) The Interpretation of the Psalms.

D. The Symbolical and Typical Interpretation of Scripture

God revealed himself not only in words, but also in facts. The two go together and are mutually complementary. The words explain the facts, and the facts give concrete embodiment to the words. The perfect synthesis of the two is found in Christ, for in Him the Word was made flesh. All the facts of the redemptive history that is recorded in the Bible center in that great fact. The various lines of the Old Testament revelation converge towards it, and those of the New Testament revelation radiate from it. It is only in their binding center, Jesus Christ, that the narratives of Scripture find their explanation. The interpreter will truly understand them only insofar as he discerns their connection with the great central fact of Sacred History.

It follows from the preceding that the expositor may not rest satisfied with a mere understanding of the Scripture narratives as such. He must discover the underlying meaning of such facts as the call of Abraham, the wrestling of Jacob, Israel's deliverance out of Egypt, the deep humiliation through which David passed before he ascended the throne. Full justice must be done to the symbolical and typical character of

Israel's history. Moreover, in the interpretation of the biblical miracles, it should not be forgotten that they are closely connected with the work of redemption. In some cases, they symbolize the redemptive work of Christ; in others they prefigure the blessings of the coming age. In a word, the interpreter must determine the significance of the facts of history as a part of God's revelation of redemption.

1. Facts May Have Symbolical Significance. Historical facts or events may serve as symbols of spiritual truth. A symbol (from *sun* and *ballo*) is not an image, but a sign of something else. And that is what the narratives of Scripture are in many instances. A couple of examples may illustrate this. Take the wrestling of Jacob, revealed in Gen. 32:24-32, and referred to in Hosea 12:2-4. What is the meaning of this incident? This is not understood until it is contemplated as a symbol of the fact that Jacob, though heir of the promises of God, had all along wrestled with God and sought to attain success in his own strength and by his own devices, and was now taught, by being disabled, that his career of self-help and resistance to God was futile; and that he had to resort to the use of spiritual weapons, particularly the weapon of prayer, in order to obtain the blessing of Jehovah. His strength had to be broken, that the power of God might become manifest in him.

Or, take one of the miracles of the Saviour. According to John 6:1-13, Jesus miraculously fed a multitude of more than 5000. To regard this miracle merely as a proof of the Lord's omnipotence is to miss the point as much as the Jews did in Jesus' day. They lost sight of the fact that it was a sign, pointing to the sufficiency of Jesus, as the heavenly bread, to satisfy the hungry souls of men. Christ himself clearly reveals the significance of this miracle in his discourse at Capernaum on the following day. The Scriptural miracles are often symbols

of spiritual truth.   The very name *semeia* points to that, and
some of the Gospel passages indicate it very clearly.   Cf. John
9:1-7, esp. vs. 5; 11:17-44, esp. vss. 25,26.

2. FACTS MAY HAVE TYPICAL SIGNIFICANCE.   When Abraham offered up his only son on Mount Moriah, he performed
a typical deed.   David, as theocratic king, was clearly a type
of his great son.   The serpent lifted up in the desert pointed
forward to the elevation of Christ on the cross.   And the high
priest entering the inner sanctuary once a year to make atonement for the sin of the people pre-figured Him who in the
fulness of time entered the heavenly sanctuary with his own
blood, thus obtaining an eternal redemption.   In connection
with the types, which occupy an important place in the Bible,
two questions arise: (a) What is a type? and (b) What rules
apply in its interpretation?

a. *The characteristics of types.*   What is a type?   A correct
answer to this question will safeguard us against the double
error of limiting the typical element too much, on the one
hand, and, on the other, of enlarging it unduly.   The word
"type" (Greek *tupos,* derived from the verb, *tupto*), denotes
(1) the mark of a blow; (2) an impression, the stamp made
by a die—hence a figure, an image; and (3) an example or
pattern, which is the most common meaning in the Bible. Both
types and symbols are indicative of something else.   They differ, however, in important points.   A symbol is a sign, while
a type is a pattern or image of something else.   A symbol may
refer to something either past, present, or future, while a type
always prefigures some future reality.   Davidson says: "A
symbol is a fact that teaches a moral truth.   A type is a fact
that teaches a moral truth and predicts some actual realization
of that truth" (*Old Testament Prophecy,* p. 229). Scriptural
types are not all of one kind.   There are typical persons, typical places, typical things, typical rites and typical facts.   Ac-

cording to Terry, the fundamental idea is that of "the preordained representative relation which certain persons, events, and institutions of the Old Testament bear to corresponding persons, events, and institutions in the New" (*Biblical Hermeneutics,* p. 246).

The following three characteristics are generally given by writers on typology: (1) There must be some notable real point of resemblance between a type and its antitype. Whatever differences there may be, the former should be a true picture of the latter in some particular point. (2) The type must be designed by divine appointment to bear a likeness to the anti-type. Accidental similarity between an Old and New Testament person or event does not constitute the one a type of the other. There must be some Scriptural evidence that it was so designed by God. This is not equivalent to the position of Marsh, who insisted on it that nothing should be regarded as typical that was not expressly so designated in the New Testament. If this canon were correct, why not apply it also to Old Testament prophecies? (3) A type always prefigures something future. Moorehead correctly says: "A Scriptural type and predictive prophecy are in substance the same, differing only in form" (Article, *"Type,"* in *The International Standard Bible Encyclopaedia*). This distinguishes it from a symbol. It is well to bear in mind, however, that the Old Testament types were at the same time symbols that conveyed spiritual truths to contemporaries, for their symbolical meaning must be understood before their typical meaning can be ascertained.

b. *The interpretation of types.* In the interpretation of symbols and types, the same general rules apply that govern the interpretation of parables. Hence we may refer to these. But there are certain special considerations that ought to be borne in mind.

(1) The interpreter should guard against the mistake of regarding a thing that is in itself evil as a type of what is good and pure. There must be congruity. It jars our moral sense to find the clothes of Esau, in which Jacob was dressed, when he deceived his father and received the blessing, represented as a type of the righteousness with which Christ adorns his saints. Of course, there are types *in malam partem* of similar antitypes. Cf. Gal. 4:22-31.

(2) The Old Testament types were, at the same time, symbols and types; because they were, first of all, symbols expressive of spiritual truth. The truth represented by these symbols for contemporaries was the same as that which they prefigured as types, though in its future realization that truth was raised to a higher level. Hence the proper way to the understanding of a type lies through the study of the symbol. The question must be settled first of all of what moral or spiritual truth the Old Testament symbols conveyed to the Israelites. And only after this is answered satisfactorily should the expositor proceed to the further query as to how this truth was realized on a higher plane in the New Testament. Thus the proper limits of the interpretation of the type will be fixed at once. To reverse the process, and begin with the New Testament realization, leads to all kinds of arbitrary and fanciful interpretations. For example, some interpreters found in the fact that the brazen serpent was made of an inferior metal, a figure of Christ's outer meanness or humble appearance; in its solidity, a sign of his divine strength; and in its dim lustre, a prefiguration of the veil of his human nature.

(3) But, having learned from a study of their symbolical import the proper limits of the types, the exact truth which they conveyed to the Old Testament people of God, the interpreter will have to turn to the New Testament for a real insight into the truth that was typified. It is patent that the

types present the truth in a veiled form, while the New Testament realities dispel the shadows and make the truth stand forth with undimmed lustre. If the prophecies can be fully understood only in the light of their fulfilment, this also applies to the types. Notice how much additional light the Epistle to the Hebrews sheds on the truths embodied in the tabernacle and its furniture.

(4) It is a fundamental principle that types, which are not of a complex nature, have but one radical meaning. Hence the interpreter is not at liberty to multiply its significations, and to make, for example, the passage of the Red Sea, regarded as a type of baptism, refer (a) to the atoning blood of Christ, which offers a safe way to the heavenly Canaan, and (b) to the trials through which Christ leads his people to their eternal rest. At the same time, it should be borne in mind that some types may find more than one fulfilment in New Testament realities, for instance, one in Christ, and another in the people who are organically connected with him. God's dwelling among Israel was a type of his tabernacling among men in Christ, and of his dwelling in the congregation of his saints. The two ideas are fundamentally one, and therefore exactly in line with each other.

(5) Finally, it is necessary to have due regard to the essential difference between type and antitype. The one represents truth on a lower, the other, the same truth on a higher stage. To pass from the type to the antitype is to ascend from that in which the carnal preponderates to that which is purely spiritual, from the external to the internal, from the present to the future, from the earthly to the heavenly. Rome loses sight of this when it finds the antitype of the Old Testament sacrifices, in the mass; of the priesthood, in the apostolic succession of priests and bishops; and of the high priest, in the pope.

EXERCISE: What was the symbolical meaning of the following? The pillars of cloud and fire (Ex. 13:21); the story of Israel's unbelief and rejection at Kadesh-Barnea (Num. 14); the crossing of Jordan (Jos. 3); the resurrection of the dry bones (Ezek. 37: 1-14); the marriage of Hosea (Hos. 1); Joshua clothed with filthy garments (Zech. 3); the cleansing of the temple (John 2:13-25); the healing of the man born blind (John 9); the raising of Lazarus (John 11); the gift of tongues (Acts 2).

What was the typical significance of the following? The passover; the tabernacle; the altar of burnt-offering; the golden candlestick; the high priest; the sabbath; the special ceremony on the Day of Atonement; Moses; Joshua; David; Solomon.

LITERATURE: Fairbairn, *Typology;* Moorehead, *Studies in the Mosaic Institutions;* Schouten, *De Tabernakel, Gods Heiligdom bij Israel;* White, *Christ in the Tabernacle;* Newton, *The Tabernacle;* Atwater, *Sacred Tabernacle of the Hebrews;* Terry *Biblical Hermeneutics,* pp. 244-303; and various works on Archaeology.

E. The Interpretation of Prophecy

In the study of prophecy, the expositor encounters some of the most difficult problems of interpretation. These result partly from the character of prophecy as such, and partly from the form in which it is often cast. There are two opposite views of prophecy that should be carefully avoided. The one is that advanced by Butler and adopted by many sects in the present day, viz., that "prophecy is nothing but the history of events before they come to pass." On this standpoint, prophecy must be studied like Sacred History, and its literal fulfilment may confidently be expected. The other view is that of many Rationalists, viz., that predictive prophecy is simply the fruit of an intuition or divination, such as often characterizes great statesmen. Extremists even deny the existence of such prophecy outright, and regard apparent cases of it as *vaticinia post eventum* (predictions after the fact). *Prophecy may simply be defined as the proclamation of that which God revealed.*

The prophet received special revelations from God, and, in turn, conveyed them to the people. These revelations served to explain the past, to elucidate the present, and to disclose the future. Their interest always centered in the Kingdom of God, or the work of redemption through Christ. The prophets received insight into the council of God through dreams, visions, inward suggestions, or oral communications; and they communicated their message to the people either by simple declarations or by a description of their dreams and visions, or by symbolical actions. Two points call for special consideration: (1) The special characteristics of prophecy; and (2) Rules for the interpretation of prophecy.

1. SPECIAL CHARACTERISTICS OF PROPHECY. The following are the most important peculiarities, which the interpreter should bear in mind.

a. *Prophecy as a whole has an organic character.* It is equally absurd to deny the predictive element altogether, and to regard prophecy merely as a collection of aphoristic predictions. The prophets do not always predict particular facts, but often promulgate general ideas that are gradually realized. Some of the most important prophecies are first couched in general terms, but in the course of God's progressive revelation increase in definiteness and particularity, as we note in those of a Messianic character. They remind one of the bud that gradually opens into a beautiful flower.

b. *Prophecy is closely connected with history.* In order to be understood, it must be seen in its historical setting. The prophets had, first of all, a message for their contemporaries. They were watchmen on the walls of Zion, to guide the destinies of ancient people of God, and to guard against the dangers of apostacy. It is a mistake, of frequent occurrence in the past, to regard the prophets as abstract personalities that were not in living contact with their environment. At present, the pendulum is swinging in the opposite direction, and it becomes necessary to warn against the idea that history will explain everything in the prophets. The ancient seer often found historical occasions transcending the limits of history.

c. *Prophecy has its own peculiar perspective.* The element of time is a rather negligible quantity in the prophets. While designations of time are not altogether wanting, their number is exceptionally small. The prophets compressed great events into a brief space of time, brought momentous movements close together in a temporal sense, and took them in at a single glance. This is called "the prophetic perspective," or, as Delitzsch calls it, "the foreshortening of the prophet's horizon." They looked upon the future as the traveler does upon a mountain range in the distance. He fancies that one mountain-top rises up right behind the other, when in reality they are miles apart. Cf. the prophecies respecting the Day of the Lord, and the twofold coming of Christ.

d. *Prophecies are often conditional,* i.e., their fulfilment is in many cases dependent on the contingent actions of men. Some scholars ascribed a conditional character to all predictions, and found in this a ready explanation for the non-fulfilment of a large number. But this is an erroneous view. This conditional character can only be ascribed to those prophecies that referred to the near future, and that could, therefore, be made conditional on the free actions of the prophet's contemporaries. It follows from the nature of the case that prophecies referring to the distant future are not so conditioned. It should be borne in mind that a prophecy may be conditional, though the condition is not expressed. Cf. Jer. 26:17-19; I Kings 21:17-29; Jonah 3:4, 10.

e. *Though the prophets often express themselves symbolically, it is erroneous to regard their language as symbolical throughout.* They did not, as some writers on prophecy supposed, construct a sort of symbolical alphabet to which they habitually resorted in the expression of their thoughts. Even P. Fairbairn falls into this error when he says that "in the prophecies of the Old Testament and the Book of Revelation, nations are a common designation for worldly kingdoms, stars for ruling powers, roaring and troubled seas for tumultuous nations, trees for the higher, as grass for the lower grades of society, running streams for the means of life and refreshment, etc." (*On Prophecy,* p. 143). It is safer to take the position of Davidson: "When Joel speaks of locusts, he means those creatures. When he speaks of the sun, moon and stars, he means these bodies. When he says, 'How do the beasts groan?' he means the beasts, and not, as Hengstenberg thinks, the uncovenanted nations of the heathen world" (*Old Testament Prophecy,* p. 171). When the prophets do express themselves symbolically, the context will usually indicate it. Sometimes it is expressly stated, as it is in Dan. 8 and Rev. 17. *As a rule the language of the prophets should be understood literally.* Exceptions to this rule must be warranted by Scripture.

f. *The prophets clothed their thoughts in forms derived from the dispensation to which they belonged,* i.e., from the life, constitution, and history of their own people. In view of this fact the question naturally arises as to whether the form was essential, so that the prophecy was destined to be fulfilled in the exact terms in which it was uttered. While it was but natural that prophecies referring to the near future should be realized in all particulars, it is by no means self-evident that this should also be the case with prophecies that point to some future dispensation. The presumption is that, after the forms of life have undergone radical changes, no more can be expected than a realization of the essential central idea. In fact, the New Testament clearly proves that a literal fulfilment is not to be expected in all cases, and that in some important prophecies the dispensational form must be stripped off. Hence it is precarious to assume that a prophecy is not fulfilled as long as the outer details are not realized. Cf. Isa. 11:10-16; Joel 3:18-21; Micah 5:5-8; Zech. 12:11-14; Amos 9:11,12, Acts 15:15-17.

g. Under the guidance of the Holy Spirit, *the prophets occasionally transcended their historical and dispensational limitations, and spoke in forms that pointed to a more spiritual dispensation in the future.* In such cases the prophetic horizon was enlarged, they sensed something of the passing character of the old forms, and gave ideal descriptions of the blessings of the New Testament Church. This feature is more common in the later than in the earlier prophets. Cf. Jer. 31:31-34; Mal. 1:11.

h. *Sometimes the prophets revealed the word of the Lord in prophetical actions.* Isaiah walked bare-footed through the streets of Jerusalem; Jeremiah hastened to the Euphrates to hide his girdle; Ezekiel lay 390 days on his left, and 40 days on his right side, bearing the iniquity of the people; and Hosea married a wife of whoredoms. Some interpreters proceed on the assumption that these actions were not real, but took place in a vision.

2. INTERPRETATION OF PROPHECY. To the preceding remarks respecting the character of prophecy, we add a few rules for its interpretation.

a. *The words of the prophets should be taken in their usual literal sense, unless the context or the manner in which they are fulfilled clearly indicate that they have a symbolical meaning.* This rule is disregarded by Hengstenberg and Henderson, when they assume that Joel, in speaking of locusts, refers to a heathen people.

b. *In studying the figurative descriptions that are found in the prophets, the interpreter should make it his aim to discover the fundamental idea expressed.* When Isaiah pictures wild and domesticated animals as dwelling together in peace and led by a little child, he gives a poetic description of the peace that will prevail on earth in the future.

c. *In the interpretation of the symbolical actions of the prophets, the interpreter must proceed on the assumption of their reality, i.e., of their occurrence in actual life, unless the connection clearly proves the contrary.* Some commentators have too hastily inferred from a supposed moral or physical impossibility, that they merely occur in a vision. Such a procedure does violence to the plain sense of the Bible.

d. *The fulfilment of some of the most important prophecies is germinant, i.e., they are fulfilled by instalments, each fulfilment being a pledge of that which is to follow.* Hence while it is a mistake to speak of a double or treble sense of prophecy, it is perfectly correct to speak of a two or threefold fulfilment. It is quite evident, e.g., that Joel's prophecy in 2:28-32 was not completely fulfilled on the day of Pentecost. Notice also the predictions respecting the coming of the Son of Man in Matt. 24.

e. *Prophecies should be read in the light of their fulfilment, for this will often reveal depths that would otherwise have escaped the attention.* The interpreter should bear in mind, however, that many of them do not refer to specific historical events, but enunciate some general principle that may be realized in a variety of ways. If he should simply ask, in such cases, to what event the prophet refers, he would be in danger of narrowing the scope of the prediction in an unwarranted manner. *Moreover, he should not proceed on the assumption that prophecies are always fulfilled in the exact form in which they were uttered. The presumption is that, if they are fulfilled in a later dispensation, the dispensational form will be disregard in the fulfilment.*

LITERATURE: Fairbairn, *On Prophecy;* Elliott, *Old Testament Prophecy;* Gloag, *Messianic Prophecy;* Riehm, *Messianic Prophecy;* Edersheim, *Prophecy and History in Relation to the Messiah;* Davidson, *Old Testament Prophecy;* Girdlestone, *The Grammar of Prophecy;* Kirkpatrick, *The Doctrine of the Prophets;* Aalders, *De Profeten des Ouden Verbonds;* Terry, *Biblical Hermeneutics,* pp. 313-337.

F. The Interpretation of the Psalms

The Psalms, the sacred songs of Israel, also form a part of the Word of God. They comprise both lyric and didactic poetry. In the didactic psalms, God gives instruction through the poet and addresses himself to the understanding; in the lyric, He reveals himself through the emotions and spiritual experiences of the sacred poets, and directs himself to the heart. The present discussion concerns itself primarily with the interpretation of the lyric psalms, which constitute by far the greatest part of our collection.

1. NATURE OF THE PSALMS. In these psalms, the poet gives utterance to his deepest experiences and emotions of joy and sorrow, hope and fear, gladsome expectation and bitter disappointment, childlike confidence and grateful recognition. He expresses his innermost feelings and lifts up his soul to God. It is often said that, while in other parts of Scripture God speaks to man, in the psalms the relation is reversed, and man speaks to God. But, while there is an element of truth in this statement, and the psalms are far more subjective than other portions of the Bible, this does not imply that the psalms are not an essential part of the Word of God. In order to understand how God reveals himself in these sacred songs, it will be necessary to have some knowledge of lyric poetry and of lyrical inspiration.

Lyric poetry contains, in the first place, *an individual element*. The poets sing of their own historical circumstances and of their personal experiences. This is quite evident from the superscriptions of the psalms. Cf. Pss. 3, 6, 7, 18, 30, etc. It is also apparent from the contents of many psalms. But these experiences, though personal, yet have *a representative character.* In the innermost recesses of his soul, the poet is conscious of his solidarity with mankind as a whole, and feels the pulse of the communal life of man. And the song that is born of this consciousness is a song which, in its crescendoes and diminuendoes, interprets the joy and sorrow, not only of the poet, but of man in general. And in view of the fact that this communal life has its fountain-head in God, the lyrical poet descends to still greater depths, or mounts to ever loftier heights, until he rests in God, in whom the life of humanity originates and who controls its joy and sorrow. Arising out of these depths, his song is, as it were, *born of God.*

This general principle must be borne in mind in the interpretation of the psalms. *They are in a sense universal, and transcend the personal and historical. The sacred singers are* living members of the Church of God, and are so *conscious of their unity with the Church* as a whole that their songs also embody the praises and the lamentations of the Church. And, as members of the Church, they also *feel that they are united to Him Who is its glorious Head,* Who suffers for and with it, and is the author of its joy. This explains the fact that Christ is sometimes heard in the psalms, now singing a plaintive song, and anon raising up his voice in a paean of victory. Again, the life of the poet in union with Christ also has its *fountain in God. Hence his song,* which *is also the song of the Church, finds its mainspring in God.* The result of it all is that in some of the psalms, the personal experiences of the poet are most prominent; that in others the communal life of Israel and of the Church finds expression; and in still others, the humiliated and exalted Christ is heard. In all the psalms we have the deep background to which we referred, and the interpreter must beware of viewing them superficially. He should never rest satisfied until he hears in them the voice of his God. And the fact that, in God's sight, the antithesis between sin and holiness is absolute, that He loves his Church but hates whatsoever opposes his Kingdom, will also explain the strong expressions of love and hatred that are found in the psalms.

2. RULES FOR INTERPRETATION. In connection with the foregoing, the following rules apply in the interpretation of the psalms:

a. *If there was a historical occasion for the composition of a psalm, this should be carefully studied.* Notice how this illumines the following psalms: 3, 32, 51, 63.

b. Because the psalms are far more subjective than other parts of the Bible, the psychological element is important for their correct interpretation. *The interpreter should study the character of the poet and the frame of mind in which he composed his song.* The more thoroughly David is known, the better his psalms will be understood.

c. In view of the fact that the psalms are not purely individual, but largely communal, *they must be regarded as utterances of the regenerate heart, of the life that is born from God; and the interpreter should not rest satisfied until he understands how they, too, reveal God's will.*

d. *In the interpretation of the Messianic psalms, a careful distinction must be made between psalms or parts of psalms that are directly, and those that are indirectly Messianic.* While the former, such as Pss. 2, 22, 45, 110, are directly Messianic, the latter, such as 72 and 89, apply first of all to the poet or some other Old Testament saint, and only, through him as an intervening type, in the second place, to Christ. There are also some that cannot be classed with either of these, which Binnie prefers to call "mystically Messianic psalms" in view of the fact that the true key to their interpretation is not found in the doctrine of the types, but in the mystical union of Christ and the Church. Cf. 16, 40. *Since the Messianic psalms are prophetic, special attention should be paid to the quotations from them in the New Testament, and to the New Testament realization of their predictions.*

e. *In connection with the so-called "Imprecatory Psalms," or, perhaps better, imprecations in the psalms, certain facts should be taken into consideration.*

(1) Orientals love the concrete, and therefore sometimes represent sin in the concrete form of the sinner.

(2) These imprecations embody the desire of the Old Testament saints for the vindication of the righteousness and holiness of God.

(3) They are not utterances of personal vindictiveness, but of the Church's aversion to sin, embodied in the sinner.

(4) They are, at the same time, a revelation of God's attitude to those who are hostile to Him and His Kingdom.

LITERATURE: Binnie, *The Psalms: Their History, Teachings and Use;* Robertson, *The Poetry and the Religion of the Psalms;* Murray, *Origin and Growth of the Psalms;* and the various Commentaries on the Psalms.

G. The Implied Sense of Scripture

The Bible as the Word of God contains a fulness and wealth of thought that is unfathomable. This is evident not only from its types and symbols and prophecies, but also from what it contains implicitly rather than by express assertion. Even in the case of human compositions we distinguish between what is expressed and what is implied. In writings of a superior order, it is often found that the language suggests and involves important truths that are embodied in words. Great

minds contain a wealth of knowledge, and whatever they com-
municate of it is related to and suggestive of that vast store,
so that it becomes quite possible to read between the lines. And
if this is true of the literary productions of men, it applies
much more to the infallible Word of God.

There is an important distinction, however. Man only knows
in part, and is not always conscious of what he knows. Moreover, he often fails to see the implications of what he says or
writes. It is quite possible that his words contain implications
which he did not see and to which he would not subscribe. It
may very well be that what can fairly be deduced from his explicit assertions, by means of logical inference or comparison,
lies entirely outside of his range of thought and is, in fact,
the very opposite of what he means. Hence the rule, so often
forgotten in practice, but yet essential to all fair controversy,
that "it is not allowable to charge upon an author the consequences of his statements when not expressly avowed or adopted, even although these consequences may be necessarily involved in the statements." He may not have contemplated
nor even seen them, so that he is not responsible for them, but
only for the employment of language which unintentionally
implies them. For the same reason it is not permissible to infer a writer's opinion on a certain matter from incidental expressions, used by him when the matter in question was not
under consideration. As a rule it is an unwarranted procedure, to ascribe to an author thoughts or sentiments which he
did not expressly utter in connection with the matter to which
they pertain. He who does this is guilty of *consequensmach-
erei.*

But in the case of the Word of God, these restrictions do
not apply. The knowledge of God is all-comprehending and
is always conscious knowledge. In giving man his Word, He
was not only perfectly aware of all that was said, but also of

all that this implied. He knew the inferences that are deduced from His written Word. Says Bannerman: "The consequences that are deduced from Scripture by unavoidable inference, and more largely still the consequences that are deduced from a comparison of the various Scripture statements among themselves, were foreseen by infinite wisdom in the very act of supernaturally inspiring the record from which they are inferred: and the Revealer not only knew that men would deduce such consequences, but designed that they should do so" (*Inspiration of the Scriptures,* p. 585). Therefore *not only the express statements of Scripture, but its implications as well, must be regarded as the Word of God.*

Jesus himself warrants this position. When the Sadducees came to him with a question which, in their estimation, clearly proved the untenableness of the doctrine of the resurrection, he referred them to the self-designation of Jehovah at the bush: "I am the God of Abraham, the God of Isaac, and the God of Jacob"; and deduced from it by good and necessary inference, the doctrine which they denied. Moreover, he reproved their failure to see the implication of that self-designation by saying, "Ye do err, not knowing the Scripture" (Matt. 22:29-32; Mark 12:24-27; Luke 20:37, 38). For other examples, cf. Rom. 4:5-12; I Cor. 9:8-10; I Tim. 5:17, 18; Heb. 4:5-9.

We feel warranted, therefore, in laying down the following rule: "*The deductions of doctrine made from its (the Bible's) statements on a comparison between them, if truly drawn, are as much a part of God's meaning and of His revelation — being indeed virtually contained in it, — as these statements themselves*" (Bannerman, *Inspiration of the Scriptures,* p. 587). It goes without saying that great care must be exercised in drawing such inferences from the written word. The deductions must be good, i.e., truly contained in the inspired statements from which they are ostensibly derived; and also necessary, or such as force themselves upon the mind that honestly applies itself to the interpretation of Scripture. Cf. Westminster Catechism, Art. VI.

H. Helps for the Theological Interpretation

The helps that may aid the expositor in the theological interpretation are twofold: (1) Real Parallels, or Parallels of Ideas: and (2) The Analogy of Faith, or of Scripture. Both proceed on the assumption that the Word of God is an organic unity of which all parts are mutually related, and are together subservient to the whole of God's revelation; and that, in the last analysis, the Bible is its own interpreter.

1. REAL PARALLELS, OR PARALLELS OF IDEAS. "Real parallels," says Terry, "are those similar passages in which the likeness or identity consists not in words or phrases, but in facts, subjects, sentiments, or doctrines." In their employment, the interpreter must determine, first of all, whether the passages adduced are really parallels, whether they are, not merely somewhat similar, but essentially identical. For instance, Prov. 22:2 and 29:13, though they reveal a certain similarity and are often regarded as parallels, are not true parallels. Parallels of ideas may be divided into two classes, *historical* and *didactic parallels*. To these may be added the quotations from the Old Testament in the New, which are also, in a sense, parallel passages.

a. *Historical Parallels.* These may be of different kinds:

(1) There are some in which a history is narrated in the same words and with the same attendant circumstances, though possibly differing slightly in matters of detail. They are valuable for mutual confirmation. Compare I Kings 22:29-35 with II Chron. 18:28-34; and Luke 22:19, 20 with I Cor. 11:24, 25.

(2) Again, there are passages in which the same narratives are couched in different words, and the circumstances are more detailed in one instance than in the other. In these cases, it is but natural to expect that the more circumstantial narrative will illumine the other. Compare Matt. 9:1-8 with Mark 2:1-12.

(3) Furthermore, there are narratives which are undoubtedly identical, but which occur in connections that are altogether different. They are most numerous in the Gospels. In such instances, the one most likely gives the true historical setting, and, insofar, sheds light on the other. Compare Matt. 8:2-4 with Mark 1:40-45 and Luke 5:12-16; and Matt. 11:6-19 with Luke 7:31-35.

(4) Finally, there are passages that do not duplicate a certain, but add an additional circumstance, and are therefore, in a way, complementary. Compare Gen. 32:24-32 with Hosea 12:4, 5.

b. *Didactic Parallels.* Here again we meet with different kinds:

(1) There are cases in which the same subject is treated, but not in the same terms. Compare Matt. 10:37 with Luke 14:26. Many interpreters attenuate the meaning of the word "hate" used by Luke, by means of the passage found in Matthew; and appeal to Matt. 6:24 to prove that the verb "to hate" may simply mean "to love less." The correctness of this interpretation may well be doubled, however. The "spiritual sacrifices" of which Peter speaks in Pet. 2:5 find a partial explanation in Rom. 12:1, which, in turn, is explained by Rom. 6:19.

(2) Then there are parallel passages that correspond in thought and expression, but of which the one has no direct connection with the preceding or following context. Thus, in Matt. 7:13, 14, the words, "Enter ye at the strait gate . . .,"

occur without any historical setting. This is supplied, however, in Luke 13:23, 24. Compare also Matt. 7:7-11 with Luke 11:5-13.

(3) Finally, there are also parallels that occur in connections entirely different, though perhaps equally fitting. It is even possible that the occasion for the statement is not the same in both places. The same saying may have been uttered on various occasions. Compare Matt. 7:21-23 with Luke 13: 25-28; and Matt. 13:16, 17 with Luke 10:23, 24.

c. *Quotations from the Old Testament in the New.* These are parallels in a certain sense. They deserve special mention, because many scholars in the present day do not hesitate to say that the writers of the New Testament, in quoting the Old, often proceeded very arbitrarily. Says Immer: "But far more numerous are those citations which treat the Old Testament arbitrarily, and in which either no relationship or only a very remote one, can be found between the thought of the New Testament writer and that of the original passage. We distinguish citations in which the agreement is only apparent and rests on the mere language; citations in which agreement is attained only by the pressing of a single word contrary to the sense; and finally citations in which the Old Testament passage could be drawn to the present thought only through the application of an unlimited allegorizing and typologizing" (*Hermeneutics,* p. 172). This statement is based on an erroneous view of the Bible as a whole, of the prophetico-typical relation of the Old Testament to the New, and of the implied sense of Scripture. The quotations in the New Testament do not all serve the same purpose.

(1) *Some serve the purpose of showing that Old Testament predictions, whether direct or indirect, were fulfilled in the New Testament.* This is true of all the prophetic passages that are introduced with the formula, "in order that it might

be fulfilled" and of several others. Cf. Matt. 2:17, 23; 4:14, 15; John 15:25; 19:36; Heb. 1:13.

(2) *Others are quoted for the establishment of a doctrine.* In Rom. 3:9-19, Paul quotes several passages from the Psalms to prove the universal depravity of man. Again, in 4:3 ff. he cites the example of Abraham, and several statements of David to prove that man is justified by faith rather than by the works of the law. Cf. also Gal. 3:6 and Heb. 4:7.

(3) *Still others are cited to refute and rebuke the enemy.* Jesus quotes Scripture in John 5:39, 40 to expose the inconsistency of the Jews, when they claimed great reverence for the Scriptures, and yet did not believe in Him of whom these testified. Notice also how he employed Scripture against them in Matt. 22:29-32; 41:46; John 10:34-36.

(4) *Finally, there are some that are cited for rhetorical purposes, or for the purpose of illustrating some truth.* In these, little regard is had to the connection in which they occur in the Old Testament, and it often seems as if they are used arbitrarily. Hence, these especially serve as a target for Rationalistic attacks. But the assaults are entirely unwarranted in view of the purpose for which they are quoted. In Rom. 10:6-8, the apostle adapts the language of Moses (Deut. 30:12-14), to his purpose. In Rom. 8:36, he applies to suffering Christians in general a word which the Psalmist wrote with reference to others long before (Ps. 44:22). And in I Tim. 5:18, he quotes the Old Testament regulation respecting the ox that treadeth out the grain, as an instructive parallel, and leaves it to his readers to deduce, by an inference *a minori ad majus,* the lesson that the human laborer is still more worthy of his hire.

2. THE ANALOGY OF FAITH, OR OF SCRIPTURE. The term "Analogy of Faith" is derived from Rom. 12:6, where we read: "Having then gifts, differing according to the grace that

is given unto us, whether prophecy, let us prophesy according to the proportion of faith (*kata ten analogian tes pisteos*)." Some commentators mistakenly interpreted "faith" objectively here, in the sense of *doctrine,* and looked upon *analogian* as the designation of an external standard. Correctly interpreted, however, the whole expression simply means, *according to the measure of your subjective faith.* Hence the term, as derived from this passage, is based on a misunderstanding.

When the early Church Fathers spoke of the *Analogia or Regula Fidei,* they meant the general principles of faith, of which several summaries were given. In course of time the name was applied to the creeds that were accepted by the Church, as, for instance, the creed of Nicea. The Roman Catholic Church even honored tradition as the rule of faith. But this is a mistaken use of the term. It is perfectly ridiculous to raise the Confessions of the Church to the dignity of *Regulae Veritatis,* for it makes that which is derived from Scripture a test of the truth of Scripture. The analogy of faith, rightly understood, is found in the Bible itself. Cellerier, in his *Hermeneutics,* speaks of two superior and two inferior degrees of this analogy, but at the same time declares that the inferior degrees are really not worthy of the name.

a. *There are two degrees of the analogy of faith with which the interpreter of the Bible is concerned.*

(1) *Positive Analogy.* The first and most important of these is the positive analogy, which is immediately founded upon Scriptural passages. It consists of those teachings of the Bible that are so clearly and positively stated, and supported by so many passages, that there can be no doubt of their meaning and value. Such truths are those of the existence of a God of infinite perfection, holy and righteous, but also merciful and gracious; of the providential rule of God and his beneficial purpose of the existence and heinousness of sin; of

the redeeming grace revealed in Jesus Christ; and of a future life and retribution.

(2) *General Analogy.* The second degree is called the general analogy of faith. It does not rest on the explicit statements of the Bible, but on the obvious scope and import of its teachings as a whole, and on the religious impressions they leave on mankind. Thus it is plain that the spirit of the Mosaic law as well as of the New Testament is inimical to human slavery. It is also perfectly clear that the Bible is hostile to pure formalism in religion, and makes for spiritual worship.

These two degrees of the analogy of faith constitute a standard of interpretation. As a connoisseur, in judging a masterpiece of painting, fixes his attention, first of all, on the central object of interest, and considers the details in their relation to this; so the interpreter must study the particular teachings of the Bible in the light of its fundamental truths.

b. *The analogy of faith will not always have the same degree of evidential value and authority.* This will depend on four factors.

(1) *The number of passages that contain the same doctrine.* The analogy is stronger when it is founded on twelve, than when it is based on six passages.

(2) *The unanimity or correspondence of the different passages.* The value of the analogy will be in proportion to the agreement of the passages on which it is founded.

(3) *The clearness of the passage.* Naturally, an analogy that rests wholly, or, to a great extent, on obscure passages, is of very dubious value.

(4) *The distribution of the passages.* If the analogy is founded on passages derived from a single book, or from a few writings, it will not be as valuable as when it is based on passages of both the Old and the New Testaments, dating from various times, and coming from different authors.

c. *When employing the analogy of faith in the interpretation of the Bible, the interpreter should bear the following rules in mind.*

(1) *A doctrine that is clearly supported by the analogy of faith cannot be contradicted by a contrary and obscure passage.* Think of I John 3:6, and the general teaching of the Bible that believers also sin.

(2) *A passage that is neither supported nor contradicted by the analogy of faith may serve as the positive foundation for a doctrine, provided it is clear in its teaching. Yet the doctrine so established will not have the same force as one that is founded on the analogy of faith.*

(3) *When a doctrine is supported by an obscure passage of Scripture only, and finds no support in the analogy of faith, it can only be accepted with great reserve.* Possibly, not to say probably, the passage requires a different interpretation than the one put upon it. Cf. Rev. 20:1-4.

(4) *In cases where the analogy of Scripture leads to the establishment of two doctrines that appear contradictory, both doctrines should be accepted as Scriptural in the confident belief that they resolve themselves into a higher unity.* Think of the doctrines of predestination and free will, of total depravity and human responsibility.

GENERAL INDEX

Allegorical interpretation, 16, 19.

Alexandria, school of, 17.

Analogy of faith or of Scripture, 163; positive analogy, 164; general analogy, 165f.; use of in interpretation, 166.

Anselm, of Laon, 24.

Antioch, school of, 20.

Aquinas, Thomas, 25.

Augustine, 22.

Authors of scriptural books, as objects of special study: their personal character, 115ff.; the social, political, and religious circumstances of their life, 119ff.; their readers and their purpose in writing, 124ff.; to be distinguished from the speakers introduced, 118f.

Autographa, inspiration of, 50ff.

Baur, F. C. and Tuebingen school, 35.

Beck, his pneumatic method of interpretation, 38.

Bible, unity of, 53; variety in, 54ff.; meaning of its separate books in the organism of Scripture, 138ff.

Bible and tradition in the Middle Ages, 23.

Cabbalistic interpretation, 17.

Calvin, his principles of interpretation, 27.

Chrysostom, John, his type of exegesis, 21.

Clement of Alexandria, and the allegorical method of interpretation, 19f.

Coccejus, his principles of interpretation, 29f.

Commentaries, correct use of, 111.

Confessionalism, exegesis in bondage to dogmatics, 28f.

Context, its importance in exegetical study to determine the exact meaning of words, 174ff.; may be of different kinds, 105ff.

Course of thought in a whole section, necessity of studying this, 99.

Erasmus, importance of for the study of the New Testament, 25f.

Farrar, on method of Coccejus, 30.

Figures of speech, abundance of in Scripture: different kinds of, 82 ff. how to determine whether a word is used figuratively, 84f.; interpretation of figures of speech, 85ff.

Fourfold sense of Scripture, popular in the early church, 20, 24.

Gematria, 17.

Germar, and his pan-harmonic interpretation, 38.

Glossae and Catenae in the Middle Ages, 24.

Grammatical-Historical method, 33f.

Grammatical school, 33.

Haggadah, 15.

Halakhah, 15.

Hapax legomena, 70f.

Helps: internal, for the explanation of words, 77ff.; for determining figurative use of words, 84f.; for the interpretation of thought, 103